Breaking Down the Schoolhouse Doors

Also by Stephen V. Newton
*Leading from the Trenches: What It Takes to
Become an Instructional Leader*

Breaking Down the Schoolhouse Doors

A Successful Transition into the Teaching Profession

Stephen V. Newton

ROWMAN & LITTLEFIELD
Lanham • Boulder • New York • London

Published by Rowman & Littlefield
An imprint of The Rowman & Littlefield Publishing Group, Inc.
4501 Forbes Boulevard, Suite 200, Lanham, Maryland 20706
www.rowman.com

6 Tinworth Street, London SE11 5AL, United Kingdom

Copyright © 2018 by Stephen V. Newton

All rights reserved. No part of this book may be reproduced in any form or by any electronic or mechanical means, including information storage and retrieval systems, without written permission from the publisher, except by a reviewer who may quote passages in a review.

British Library Cataloguing in Publication Information Available

Library of Congress Cataloging-in-Publication Data
Names: Newton, Stephen V., author.
Title: Breaking down the schoolhouse doors : a successful transition into the teaching profession / Stephen V. Newton.
Description: Lanham, Maryland : Rowman & Littlefield, [2018]
Identifiers: LCCN 2018035902 (print) | LCCN 2018038023 (ebook) | ISBN 9781475843798 (electronic) | ISBN 9781475843774 (cloth : alk. paper) | ISBN 9781475843781 (pbk. : alk. paper)
Subjects: LCSH: Student teachers—Training of. | Teaching—Vocational guidance.
Classification: LCC LB2157.A3 (ebook) | LCC LB2157.A3 N49 2018 (print) | DDC 370.71/1—dc23
LC record available at https://lccn.loc.gov/2018035902

™ The paper used in this publication meets the minimum requirements of American National Standard for Information Sciences—Permanence of Paper for Printed Library Materials, ANSI/NISO Z39.48–1992.

Contents

Preface		vii
Introduction		1
1	The Educational Landscape	5
2	You Are the Brand Name	17
3	Reinventing Yourself	29
4	Finding Your Voice	41
5	Learn Your Craft (or Find Another)	53
6	The Power of a Reflective Notebook	67
7	Building a Better Portfolio	79
8	The Application Process	91
9	Interview Preparation	103
10	Mastering the Interview	115
11	The Final Analysis	127
About the Author		139

Preface

Nearly a decade ago, a university professor asked me if I'd speak to a group of education majors about the realities of teaching from a school administrator's perspective. At the time, I was happy to oblige but was immediately stunned by the response from the students. I made the mistake of assuming that preservice teachers had a strong grasp of the profession in generalized ways and I might simply add some nuance to the conversation.

In reality, it was clear that preservice teachers were highly motivated and intelligent young people who desperately lacked insight into the very profession they were pursuing. This was a problem that demanded a solution.

Trying to establish the best way to fill the void was not an easy work in the beginning. I was uncertain about which skills teachers should learn in their preparation courses and which skills were part of the very reason they engage in student teaching. The gaps I noticed were not an indictment against any group or the work they were conducting with teachers.

As the years passed and as I continued to be asked to conduct a version of my first speaking engagement, the focus of my work evolved. Despite the hard work the teachers put into their college studies, they were unable to grasp certain concepts. The world of teaching was beyond their current set of life experiences. They wanted to do well in their chosen profession and were eager to learn.

From my professional perspective, I appreciated their desire to be better prepared. However, I also recognized that waiting to teach them important skills for success in the classroom until they were on the job was not a wise approach.

I also noticed that many preservice teachers squandered the powerful experience of student teaching because they lacked focus and direction on maximizing the opportunity. What is worse is that they did not know the difference.

Without guidance and mentoring on all aspects of the profession, teachers cannot be expected to engage at the highest levels. In essence, we send them the message that they should do their best in a role that is very poorly defined.

I believe that we can do better than this. Our students desperately need teachers of the highest caliber we can produce and we cannot afford to wait several years for the teacher to figure things out through trial and error. As a profession, we also must acknowledge that we have failed to capture some of our strongest talent because we have not clearly described how to be successful in entering the profession. To the degree that amazing teachers cannot find work, we have failed to help them enter the profession.

This work is the culmination of years of my working with student teachers to assess their misconceptions, skill gaps, and common mistakes. My hope is that this book will be a useful tool for anyone entering the profession. If it serves its designed purpose, talented and committed teachers will join us in the profession much better prepared and be able to assist in helping our students.

Introduction

Teaching is a life committed to service. When young people decide to pursue this profession, they are committing to a career for helping others. The field of education certainly needs talented and dedicated teachers to guide children. The demand for quality teachers is on the rise, and many young people are responding to the call. The teaching profession is an incredibly demanding vocation but one that is equaling rewarding and fulfilling.

Earning the position of a teacher who is entrusted with a class full of children is not a guarantee. Preparatory programs simply confer a college degree and accompanying licensure. Neither of these required documents is a promise of future employment.

Novice teachers can adopt a wide range of habits and dispositions to prepare themselves adequately for a teaching position. The first step prospective teachers must take is to evaluate their professional goal and develop a strong and sensible plan to meet it. There is a fundamental difference between a goal and a plan.

People set goals in all aspects of their lives: professional goals, weight loss goals, or financial goals. In fact, people embrace each new year with a list of resolutions that represent their goals for the coming year. Before the end of January, many new year's resolutions begin to fade. As quickly as goals were made, they soon disappear. One reason this happens is that people fail to develop a strong plan to assist in the completion of their chosen goal.

Goals demand specific and discrete action steps to ensure their completion. When people fail to reach their goals in life, it is rarely because they chose the wrong goal. The underlying reason for failure is usually rooted in a poorly devised plan.

Before a teacher can develop a solid plan to meet a professional goal, the teacher needs to gain absolute clarity on the goal. Preservice teachers may mistakenly believe that their goal is to successfully complete the requirements of the student teaching experience and graduate from college. Meeting a university's list of requirements is certainly necessary to obtain licensure. However, finishing college and getting a teaching degree is not really the goal. Fundamentally, the goal for a prospective teacher is to be hired for a teaching position. That is the goal.

Several hurdles stand in the way between declaring a college major in education and being able to assume the responsibilities of a classroom teacher. Some of the hurdles like meeting college coursework requirements are quite obvious to all students. Other obstacles are less understood by prospective teachers. For example, building a high-quality set of instructional experiences during a limited amount of student teaching time is a daunting task that is not fully explained to prospective teachers. These obstacles demand a strong and thoughtful plan.

Strong action plans keep a person focused on the goal and ensure that adequate progress is being made to reach the destination. For example, hikers often enter heavily wooded areas that are relatively unknown to them. This can present a serious possibility of getting lost.

One technique that hikers use is to find a distant mountain on the skyline. Hikers will orient themselves in a way to ensure that a road lies between them and the mountain. When the hiker begins to wander around in the woods, finding a way to safety is always ensured. The hiker must simply walk toward the mountain. Because this fixed point in the distance does not move, the hiker simply walks toward it and will invariably encounter the road that lies in between.

It is important to consider that the hiker will rarely be able to walk a straight path toward the mountain. Boulders and fallen trees likely will block the desired path. The hiker will have to make constant course corrections in the short term. For short periods, the hiker may temporarily walk in a different direction than the mountain to get past an obstacle. Once the barrier has been avoided, the hiker can get a bearing back on the mountain in the distance and resume walking toward it.

The mountain is the hiker's goal. It does not move. It is a constant. The path that the hiker must take to walk toward the mountain represents the plan the hiker has devised. This is never a straight path. Some obstacles can be foreseen; others creep up without warning. The hiker makes sensible adjustments in the moment while keeping the goal in sight.

Like mountains, professional goals are always found in the distance. They usually take a long time and a considerable investment to accomplish. Prospective teachers must keep the goal in the forefront of their mind but spend their energy in navigating the immediate steps that are in front of them. If they must take small detours to get around obstacles, they must quickly reassess what their next steps must be to get lined back up with their distant goal.

Unfortunately, the actual plan for preservice teachers to follow for achieving the goal of employment has not been well illuminated. The path from student teaching to running one's own classroom is not well defined. There are many things a teacher should do to maximize the chances of attaining a teaching position. The goal has been established. The following chapters are the plan.

Chapter 1

The Educational Landscape

Many of the most difficult times in a person's life are those marked by significant transitions. Whether it is leaving the familiarity of a neighborhood elementary school to enter junior high or taking the step to live with another person in marriage, life transitions are usually both a cause of celebration and a time of significant stress and anxiety.

By choosing to devote a life to public education, new teachers must transition immediately from the role of a college student to a competent professional with precious little time to make the transformation. At first blush, new teachers appear well equipped as they have spent a significant amount of time preparing for the moment in their preparatory programs.

However, the complexities of the current educational landscape require far more from teachers than ever before. Despite the best efforts of college preparatory programs, new teachers are often ill-equipped to keep pace with the demands of both professional responsibilities and the needs of the students they serve. Even with strong preparation programs, new teachers leave the theoretical world of academic preparation and are immediately thrust into a very practical world of teaching students.

Because of the critical needs of students in today's world, the margin of error for teachers to learn by trial and error has diminished considerably. Students have always been negatively impacted as teachers learned their craft, but vulnerable students have far more to lose. There are simply more students who require consistent expertise to survive.

New teachers have a very narrow window of preservice teaching experience to hone their skills. It is nearly impossible to accrue the necessary set of skills within the limited collegiate experience. The student teaching experience can take many forms with preservice teachers experiencing a wide variety of practices. Likewise, the quality of these experiences often depends on several factors that are largely beyond their control.

Student teachers may have very little input regarding where they will receive their student teaching experience. Depending upon the availability within cooperating communities, both the city and the school within the city may be out of the teacher's control. Also, student teachers may not have much choice of who their mentor will be and which grade they will be teaching. Many of the logistics that can shape the experience they will receive is decided independent of the students' skills or interests.

If the demands upon preservice teachers exceed the preparation they receive in their preparatory work and their student teaching experience unfolds in ways largely out of their control, new teachers must take the burden upon themselves to focus their transition efforts to produce better outcomes. As bleak as this picture may seem, new teachers can invest in themselves in several targeted ways to optimize their student teaching experience and also in other preparation work to sharpen their limited skills before transitioning into the profession.

New teachers must recognize a fundamental fact about their place as they finish college. Their teacher preparation program promised them a college diploma and a teaching license. However, the program never promised the graduates a job. Teachers can easily fall prey to the expectation that one thing will lead to another and with the diploma will come an inevitable slew of job offers. For some, this may be the case. However, job fairs are full of teacher candidates who continue to press forward each year, failing to secure a viable teaching position.

There are several reasons why this may be the case. Some teachers may struggle in some aspect of their social interaction or their academic preparation that leaves them ill-equipped to secure a position. However, there are many talented and eager college graduates who are also unemployed. Despite the public shortage of school teachers, jobs remain relatively competitive and the days of weak teachers securing jobs are gone. Some schools may be desperate enough to hire a questionable candidate, but for the most part, attractive positions are often sought after by many potential teachers seeking work.

New teachers must also seek an edge to separate themselves from other candidates. This essential edge can only be developed in the few short months as college students finish their preparation and begin their student teaching experience. New teachers do not just have to be good, but they must be better. When compared to others who have received exactly the same educational experiences and preservice opportunities, new teachers must seek nuanced ways in which they can create separation from their peers and become the obvious choice for hire.

Between the critical needs of students and the competitive nature of the job market, there is no longer a place for an average teacher. New teachers must demand greatness from themselves. Employers will likely have little patience for teachers to fumble through their work and will be unlikely to invest in a teacher who may possess the potential but demonstrates little from the outset.

Novice teachers must decide if they are ready to commit to the level of expectation that this new work demands. Certainly, the work is not required. Preservice teachers can approach their work by ensuring that they meet the minimum expectations of their programs. These teachers will complete all course requirements and will receive the required signatures to meet the obligations of their program of study.

However, teachers who are committed to this new work will do all of those things plus a few more and will become far more prepared and employable than their peers. These teachers will be the ones who get to choose where they will work, and their future will not be left to chance. Teachers committed to this work will take control of their own fate and will build far more tangible skills in the same allotment of time and opportunity as their peers. They will finish poised to become employable and make an immediate impact on the lives of their students. These skills are the future of true teacher preparation.

Prior to entering the classroom for practicum and student teaching hours, the experience that most future teachers have with the classroom is the set of experiences they had themselves as students in their youth. There is a real danger in this reality as preservice teachers have just enough background knowledge of the profession to have a very skewed and limited perspective of the profession.

Young people certainly experience the reality of public school education, but it is from the distinct vantage point of the learner. Everything a student witnesses in the classroom comes from the perspective of being on the receiving end of instruction. Likewise, students have these experiences when they are young and largely unable to understand why events are unfolding as they are in the classroom setting. Regardless, students form opinions about which teachers are better and whether school is meaningful based upon an incomplete set of information about what was happening within the environment.

For example, students often have fond memories of teachers who formed strong relationships with them and believe they were great teachers. However, young people often prefer certain teachers for the wrong reasons. Popular teachers may not demand high levels of rigor in the classroom and may choose to remain popular rather than challenge students in their classroom. Students often confuse popular teachers with good teachers.

Even as students mature and are better able to recognize the true colors of their former teachers, the perspective of students is limited in another fundamental way. With rare exception, students only see the portion of teaching that happened when classes were in session. Astute preservice teachers may be able to recall and critically examine the effectiveness of their teachers, but it would only encompass the things that happened during the instructional period.

Educators recognize that a large and significant portion of the teaching experience happens before and after a class session. For example, students never get to witness the collaboration of teachers where they discuss strong instructional strategies and adjustments they intend to make in light of student performance. Similarly, students never experience the thought and deliberation that teachers go through in designing lessons and assessments in the noninstructional hours.

This reality puts preservice teachers in a place where their understanding of teaching is not understood in the larger context of related educational responsibilities and considerations. Even to the degree that a preservice teacher may be able to recognize sound instructional practices, the thinking and rationale behind these decisions are beyond the purview of all outsiders.

Because of this, preservice teachers are in constant danger of believing they know more about their chosen profession than they really do. Additionally, it is easy for prospective teachers to forget that the teachers they have known *already have jobs*. When preservice teachers attempt to analyze their own personality and teaching strengths, they often measure it against their own former teachers. However, these teachers are not currently seeking employment.

The reality is that many employed teachers may struggle greatly to secure a job if they were forced to find a new job. Keeping a job is an easier proposition than securing a job. Because marginal teachers are often able to retain their positions despite weak skills, it can give the appearance to new teachers that those levels of performance are the expectation.

In actuality, school leaders are often keenly aware of their current staff members who have weak skills and are not always able to relieve them of their duties. However, these weak teachers are a constant reminder to principals that hiring great teachers is of critical importance. Having weak teachers in a faculty often triggers exceptionally higher expectations when a principal is able to recruit and hire a new teacher.

Teachers seeking employment should not look to their weaker peers to determine what an acceptable level of performance is. Rather, new teachers must be very cautious in who they use as a professional mentor and role model. Young teachers must find the best educators within a setting to determine where they should set their own expectations for themselves.

Given the choice, school administrators will never settle for an average candidate. Although some regions and some disciplines may be in higher need of qualified candidates and the associated talent pool is a bit shallow, teacher candidates should not fool themselves into believing that weak preparation and subpar skills will be sufficient to secure a teaching position.

Preservice teachers must reevaluate their notion of good teaching and whether they possess the insight to recognize a good teacher. This can be difficult as there are strong emotional ties to the teachers in their past. This is not to suggest that the work and kindness of former teachers must be forgotten or disparaged. Rather, new teachers must simply recognize that they may know and understand far less about the profession they have chosen (and will soon enter) than they first imagined.

This is in no way an admission of defeat. In the same way that a patient in the hospital is not an expert in the work of physicians, former students are not experts at teaching by sharing the same space. Acknowledging this tendency to overestimate the particulars of a profession is a good starting point to building a stronger and more realistic vision of what it takes to be an excellent educator.

Prospective teachers should use their experiences as students as a good starting point. While they may not know the full scope of what teachers were doing, they certainly have firsthand experiences of how teachers were able to make a student feel. Every student remembers those who built them up and those who broke them down.

Every student is able to understand the incredibly strong or weak impact a teacher can make upon their lives. The information that a preservice teacher lacks is *what it takes* to create and ensure the best outcomes for their students. Learning these skills in a live environment with students is the task for preservice teachers in the very brief amount of contact time they have with students.

This small window of opportunity often quietly passes without the student teacher capturing a set of powerful experiences. However, even in this abbreviated period of time, student teachers can acquire powerful skills if their efforts are properly focused. This can create the needed advantage for a new teacher to secure a position and transition effectively into the teaching experience.

The necessary experiences that will set a new teacher apart in ways that can ensure a smooth transition into securing a teaching position revolve around the experiences as a student teacher. Prospective teachers have much to learn and consider apart from their presence in the classroom, but the most important investment they need to make in themselves largely plays out in light of their experiences with students. These experiences will occur in a very brief window of time and will play out under the tight control of the sort of experiences the mentor teacher will orchestrate.

Student teachers need to be prepared for the possibility that their mentor may not allow them to function as they wish and could limit the full breadth of professional opportunities that student teachers may desire. Student teachers must be prepared to develop a plan to invest in their own professional growth regardless of the way in which a mentor teacher intends to lead them.

Cooperating teachers undoubtedly provide an essential service to preservice teachers by hosting and mentoring them through their student teaching experience. However, student teachers must be prepared to face the reality that their host teacher may have many professional limitations.

While colleges usually strive to limit mentor teachers to highly effective teachers, this is not always the case. Moreover, even highly effective teachers have different aspects of their own professional skill set that are not as strong as other areas of practice. Additionally, many cooperating teachers are highly successful classroom teachers but may not have strong skills in mentoring others.

Simply, being a highly effective teacher requires different skills than being a highly effective mentor. Are student teachers then set up for failure from the beginning? To the contrary, prospective teachers must recognize that they must take initiative for their own learning and span all of the inevitable gaps that may be a part of their experience.

As prospective teachers receive their assignment from their college advisor, they must seek to develop a relationship with their mentor immediately. Certainly, the student teacher will rely heavily on the wisdom and insight that the mentor provides. Creating a strong and trusting professional relationship is a critical key to the success of the student teaching experience.

Student teachers must begin forging this relationship with a spirit of thankfulness. Mentor teachers do not typically receive a monetary stipend for their efforts and agreeing to host a student teacher undoubtedly requires a significant investment of time and energy from an already busy professional.

It is also important to consider that the landscape of the classroom has changed considerably in the current age of educational accountability. Many veteran educators remember that student teaching experiences in the past were often marked by the mentor teacher largely abandoning the student teacher to take over the classroom after a few weeks of observing and leading a few practice lessons.

In former days, hosting a student teacher became popular among cooperating teachers who desired an easy semester where someone else had taken over their responsibilities in the classroom. In the current educational setting, teachers are often reluctant to allow a student teacher to enter their classroom because the mentors are keenly aware that they will be expected to produce robust student achievement results despite the fact that a novice teacher instructed their students for a portion of the school year.

Consequently, current student teaching arrangements are often marked by mentor teachers who insist on longer periods of team teaching and remaining very close to the instructional process even after the student teacher has taken over the classroom.

This is not to suggest that this will make for a lesser experience for a student teacher. In fact, having a mentor teacher closely observe instruction throughout the course of the placement will likely create more opportunities for feedback and critique. Student teachers must remain flexible and find ways to capitalize on whatever role and form the mentor allows to unfold within the classroom. Student teachers must welcome and encourage a lively system of feedback to help themselves grow with every opportunity they are given. This, of course, is predicated upon a strong relationship between the mentor and student teacher.

Young teachers must recognize that it is incumbent on them to foster this relationship. For example, a mentor teacher may be shy and reserved by nature. This mentor may not offer much unsolicited feedback. Without the student teachers initiating conversation and feedback, days and weeks could easily pass by where they are completing their assigned classroom experience but may not be growing much in the process. A student teacher may not be able to control the experiences the mentor is allowing but must insist on meaningful feedback from the mentor.

Of course, this is best accomplished by acknowledging the expertise of the mentor and by asking as many questions as the mentor will tolerate within debriefing sessions. Within a trusting professional relationship, student teachers must set aside their own desire to be seen as a strong, competent teacher from the very beginning.

Regardless of academic preparation, all student teachers are novices in the act of teaching simply because they have not, by definition, had a significant amount of practice as they begin their assignment. Even mentor teachers who are reluctant to be critical will likely offer feedback if they are prompted by their student teacher approaching them with a genuine sense of humility and a desire to get better.

Young teachers can make a serious mistake if they overlook their relationship with their mentor in their excited attempts to take over a classroom. This relationship is the very foundation from which every other experience will emerge. In fact, a strong relationship with a mentor may be the way that student teachers increase the likelihood that they will be entrusted to take on more tasks than a mentor may originally be uncomfortable in allowing.

Many of the recommendations for maximizing the student teaching experience will only be possible with the blessing of the mentor. If the mentor cooperates with the creative ways to build additional skills, the innovative ideas are more likely to happen. While mentors may not be able to prevent a student teacher from excelling, they can certainly assist tremendously if they understand and support the additional efforts a student teacher is contemplating.

In ancient Hebrew, the Jewish people's word for *face* was the word *panim*. It is fascinating to note that this word is always plural. There is no singular word to describe a face. In this language, however, a plural word did not necessarily imply that there is a multiple number of something in quantity. Rather, plural words could also describe one thing with many aspects.

It is in this way that a face is plural. Indeed, in modern English, people may describe a deceitful person as being two-faced to portray a person who acts in one way to a certain group of people but presents himself in an entirely different way around another group. While this term is used to suggest negative traits in a person, it strikes upon the similar notion that people present many faces to those around them.

People may present the face of a son or daughter around their parents. In front of a significant other, an entirely different face may come to the forefront. The face of the son recedes and that of the boyfriend emerges. While the person who is both the son and the boyfriend remains the same, the face that this man puts forward is entirely different depending upon the social situation. In fact, they may be hardly recognizable to a loved one when they see the face that is normally hidden from them.

This phenomenon is what makes social interactions so clumsy and awkward when a person shares the same space for the first time with two groups of people who have only seen one of their faces. In fact, parents are often quite shocked to see their children present themselves in a manner that is foreign to the way in which they normally view their child. Of course, this is as often a pleasant surprise as it is a negative one.

In the same way that a person expresses a different face to their loved ones, a person also presents a social face in a professional setting. For most of a young person's life, their social face is that of a student. This phase can begin to emerge as early as a preschool setting and continues for thirteen consecutive years in school followed by an additional four or five as they receive a bachelor's degree. This student face is usually quite comfortable after so many years.

While young people may continue to interact as a son or daughter or even a part-time employee, they get very accustomed to their role as a student. However, the very nature of the transition the preservice teacher is making necessitates that this well-worn face be set aside.

In its place, the young person must immediately acquire another face. This is the face of a professional educator. It is important to note that, not only is this face expected to be adopted immediately upon transitioning into a student teaching experience, but it is not marked by any symbolic ceremony that denotes how important this transition point actually is.

The way in which students approach their responsibilities is fundamentally different than the way in which a professional does. That is not to say that professionals are responsible, and students are not. Students often show tremendous commitment, hard work, and pride in all that they do. Obviously, there are many professionals who could learn some of these lessons from their younger colleagues.

However, students are fundamentally different than true professionals in one important regard. The very nature of being a student is to complete a predetermined amount of work. Typically, this work is in the form of assignments and projects that students dutifully complete in sequential order over a predetermined set of time.

For students who excel in their studies, success in the classroom is marked by a commitment to getting things done by checking off important assignments from a to-do list. Certainly, professionals may also keep a to-do list as a reminder to complete various tasks in their day. However, the entirety of the student experience is based upon the completion of tasks.

Professionals, on the other hand, see their work in a different way. The job for an educator is not done when they have completed an assignment. Educators recognize that their craft is a work in progress that is constantly evolving. Educators recognize that the mastery of their profession is a lifelong journey and is not simply a sequence of events or tasks to be completed. This is one of the fundamental problems that preservice teachers encounter when they transition into the classroom for the first time.

Up to this point, a student's week is defined by attending classes for a set number of minutes, writing term papers, and putting together a presentation as a requirement for a course. Upon entering their new classroom assignment, preservice teachers often mistakenly view their day's work in the same way. Preservice teachers may view their day in this task-oriented way by focusing on ancillary issues: When must they arrive? When can they go home? Do they have to attend that collaborative team meeting? What tasks are they expected to fulfill while at school during the day?

A student asks if he is required to attend a meeting. A teacher decides to attend an optional meeting because he knows he needs to be there. On the occasions when preservice teachers transition into their student teaching placement and continue to present their *student* face, problems will naturally emerge. There is inevitable communication breakdown and dysfunction as the mentor expects their student teachers to act like professionals while the preservice teachers continue to see themselves as students.

The mentor teacher sees plenty of students throughout the day but reserves that designation for the young people sitting in desks in front of them. The mentor teacher has no interest in viewing or treating their preservice teacher as another student who needs *student-like* attention throughout the course of the day. The degree to which a preservice teacher continues to see herself as a student is the degree to which the preservice teacher will likely struggle.

The environment in which a person grows up and finds her initial belonging in this world defines her primary discourse. This is the role where people feel most comfortable and where they fully understand the social rules and norms that become the basis of how they fit into the world.

Because those entering the teaching profession tend to do so just after they finish college, they are usually young people with very little life under their belt outside of what they have learned in their primary discourse. The act of transitioning not only into the adult world but adopting a secondary discourse as a professional educator brings about several adjustments.

A new teacher must learn the new roles and norms that are associated with a professional environment. This environment has its own language, patterns of expected behaviors, and belief systems. Depending on the upbringing and life experiences of the new teacher, this professional setting may match nicely with the primary discourse that a person adopted early in life.

For example, if a young person grows up in an environment where hard work is appreciated, and success is celebrated by the development of skills, this person will likely be able to merge his primary discourse with a modern classroom that expects and demands it. A world view that embraces a growth mindset is quite natural to this person.

This is in stark contrast to a world view that values success simply as a function of innate intelligence and sees the world stage as the place where smart people prove themselves and less intelligent people continuously struggle. This young person may have a very difficult adjustment in adopting a secondary discourse that embraces the healthy academic struggle where students make slow and steady progress over time as they work diligently to grow as learners. Educators who have lived a fixed mindset to learning in their youth as part of their primary discourse will struggle mightily when the environment demands that they believe different things about student potential and promise than they ever were forced to consider.

There are many positive and healthy attributes that a person brings from his primary discourse. This can be a language of hard work, integrity, and perseverance. Unfortunately, a person's primary discourse can just as often inhibit a person from evolving a new secondary discourse that matches the demands of the profession.

Primary discourses can seep into every aspect of a person's professional life and a person must recognize that new beliefs and practices may need to be fostered to function well in the professional environment that is the young teacher's secondary discourse.

Young professionals experience this in a profound way when they begin their work in the classroom and find themselves acting and speaking in ways that would be hardly recognizable to their family and social circle of their youth. With practice, jumping back and forth between discourses can be a refreshing way to energize and reinvigorate as a person. With the pressures of performing as a consummate professional constantly, it is no doubt that young teachers desire to return home (both figuratively and literally) on occasion to feel the security and familiarity of the place in the world where their comfortable primary discourse is still the valued language.

Young teachers can certainly retain the comforts of their primary discourse but must recognize that there is great satisfaction in their developing secondary discourse as a professional educator. However, finding the same level of comfort in this world takes some time as the values of this world have simply not been practiced much in the beginning of a person's transition to the education profession.

The student teaching experience marks the time in which educators are asked to set up residence within their secondary discourse and merely vacation back in the locale of their primary discourse. This can seem painful and foreign, but a young teacher cannot underestimate the importance of letting former approaches, beliefs, and habits go in favor of the demands of the new discourse.

Chapter 2

You Are the Brand Name

Before preservice teachers begin a student teaching assignment, they should spend some time reflecting deeply upon themselves and their current state of preparation. This can be accomplished through a formal self-assessment of the characteristics of a quality teacher.

Certainly, during their college experience, they have been successful in many ways. However, academic preparation only hints at the kind of competency that a teacher must display immediately upon accepting a position. It is important to conduct a thorough self-analysis of individual strengths and weaknesses so that the limited time spent in the classroom setting can be as useful as possible.

As with any profession, young teachers will undoubtedly be stronger at some aspects of the job than others based upon their life experiences and personality type. This is not to say that preservice teachers are at a disadvantage if they recognize limited skills in a particular area. Rather, it can serve as an important reminder of the very skills they need to practice during their assignment.

This self-assessment must be based on the components of the wide variety of skills that make up the job description of a teacher. Because young teachers often only have their own former teachers as a reference point, they need to make this self-evaluation based upon something more objective and comprehensive.

Preservice teachers should research several teacher evaluation instruments to get a feel of the way in which good teaching is articulated. Online research will easily reveal a few different instruments that are available for review. Prospective teachers should also request to see the evaluation instrument that is in place for the teachers in the school where they have been assigned.

Asking a mentor teacher to review the instrument to discuss how teachers in that school interpret the categories is an excellent start to understanding the complexities of teaching. Every good evaluation instrument also contains a detailed rubric explaining the range of proficiencies a teacher may have in each category.

Beginning teachers should spend several hours poring over the nuance between the way in which a rubric describes basic skills in an area of instruction versus the additional skills needed to be considered proficient in that area.

For example, teacher evaluations will certainly comment on the ability of teachers to assess the learning of students (see Table 2.1). Within the performance rubric, an unsatisfactory teacher in this area would likely be described as follows:

> Teacher seldom assesses students and does not monitor student learning. Teacher does not give students feedback, or it is of substandard quality.

This contrasts with the way the rubric may describe teachers with basic skills in this area:

> Teacher assesses students in a sporadic fashion and partially monitors their progress. Students receive general, nonspecific feedback but remain largely unaware of how their work will be evaluated.

Preservice teachers should reflect on these two descriptors of a teacher. Obviously, there are far more proficient and distinguished behaviors to describe a master teacher, but young teachers need to begin with the humble acknowledgment that they will likely be very weak at skills they have never

Table 2.1. Assessment of Student Learning

Unsatisfactory	Basic	Proficient	Distinguished
Teacher seldom assesses students and does not monitor student learning. Teacher does not give students feedback or it is of substandard quality.	Teacher assesses students in a sporadic fashion and partially monitors their progress. Teacher gives general, nonspecific feedback but students remain largely unaware of how their work will be evaluated.	Teacher monitors student learning for groups of students only. Teacher makes students aware of criteria for success. Some students track their own learning.	Teacher weaves formative assessment through all aspects of instruction. Teacher gives individual students specific feedback. Students assess their own work and monitor their own progress.

attempted. Teachers should spend time contemplating how they can ensure that they are at least performing in a satisfactory manner.

In the previous example, there are a few distinct differences between an unsatisfactory method of assessing students and a basic set of skills. First, there is a difference in frequency that the rubric describes. Incompetent teachers seldom assess their students while developing teachers engage in assessment in a sporadic manner. This distinction should cause a teacher to reflect that frequency of assessment is important.

How much should a teacher assess students? How might a teacher incorporate assessment into classroom instruction without simply testing students all the time? These kinds of reflective questions will orient novice teachers toward the right kinds of questions that should be on the forefront of their mind as they begin leading a classroom.

Likewise, this rubric makes a distinction between teachers who do not offer quality feedback to the learner through their assessments and those who begin to recognize that specific feedback is the only way students will fix the mistakes they are making in their work. Preservice teachers should reflect *before* entering the classroom for the first time on how they intend to offer feedback to students.

Will the teacher write "Good job!" on the top of an essay and conclude that he has given the student proper feedback on the work? What should a student take away from a comment such as this? Is this sort of comment likely to inspire her to fix any mistakes she may have made in her writing? How many specific comments are likely sufficient for a five-paragraph essay?

Most college students are aware that assessing student learning is important. However, preservice teachers have not likely begun developing a plan of how that will look when they are reviewing a specific assignment they give to students. This is the transition from a theoretical understanding of teaching to a very practical one performed before a live audience.

Just as riding a bicycle is different than reading about riding a bicycle, teaching is much different than learning about teaching. Thoroughly reviewing a teacher's evaluation rubric will at least help the novice teacher focus on all the different areas of professional responsibility that must be juggled to meet expectations.

Upon conducting their first few lessons in the classroom, preservice teachers should score themselves by committing to a specific performance level for each category. For each rubric score, the teacher should list out bullet point examples justifying why that performance indicator is accurate and valid. For example, if the teacher were to mark herself basic for assessing student learning, she should include the following notes:

> I noted specific grammatical errors and sentence fragments on the essay I assigned. I conferred with students while they were writing, giving feedback in areas where they seemed stuck in their thinking.

This sort of evidence would certainly describe a teacher who is not performing in the unsatisfactory category. However, there is one additional step that is the most instructive of all for the teacher. In evaluating the rubric, the teacher should note the rubric category that most closely matches current performance but then take it a step further. The teacher should also look to the next level above and see what sort of behavior or skill is still missing that would prevent her from moving up another level.

For example, the rubric descriptor for proficiency in assessing student learning may be as follows:

Teacher assesses students on a regular basis. Students receive accurate and specific feedback. Some students engage in self-assessing their own work.

When the novice teacher reflects upon her recent classroom lesson, she should take pride that assessing students is becoming a part of daily classroom practice. However, the teacher should quickly recognize that, thus far, she has not built in any mechanism for students to self-assess their own work. This teacher should not mark herself as proficient in this area yet. However, she now has a new target for advancing her own practice in this critical area of performance.

It should be noted that this exercise was possible without any assistance or feedback from the mentor teacher or an administrator. Certainly, outside feedback would be valuable and welcomed but is not essential for a preservice teacher to advance in her craft. This is especially helpful for teachers who have not been assigned a strong mentor or for those who have mentors who do not give particularly descriptive feedback.

A new teacher must recognize that mastering the skills required of a teacher takes many years of experience and practice to hone. However, a minimum level of competency is absolutely expected from the very beginning. Many of the performance areas demand competency from the first days of the student teaching experience. All professional skills are important, but some have a level of urgency about them as well.

For example, one expectation for teachers is that they create an environment of respect and care for students. This is an expectation that the teacher will show care and concern for the well-being of students and will treat them with respect constantly. Teachers are expected to maintain emotional control when dealing with students even on the occasions when the students are misbehaving and are showing no respect for the teacher.

In these moments, and especially in these moments, teachers are required to maintain high levels of professionalism and refrain from embarrassing or humiliating students as they get the classroom back on track from student disruption. This requirement for teachers is one of the indicators that the teacher is creating and preserving an educational environment for all students at all times.

This is not always easy, but it is always expected. More importantly, this is not an area where a novice teacher is given a pass to develop adequate skills over time. Students need to be safe in their classroom every day. This cannot be unveiled in stages according to a teacher's timeline of practice and development. This quality must be intact from the first day.

This presents an exceptionally difficult challenge for preservice teachers as it is also one of the most difficult skill sets to develop. Education is a highly social environment that is often marked by complex interpersonal dynamics that do not always proceed as planned. Creating a safe and healthy environment for students may likely be one of the weakest areas of performance for a new teacher and is the one that has the smallest margin of error.

This fact should serve as a wake-up call for new teachers to embrace that they are beginners and have a lot to learn in a very short amount of time. Learning quickly is possible, but it takes great focus and concentration to practice the high leverage skills that protect the learning environment.

Other areas of teacher practice are certainly as important but do not carry with them the same urgency to implement. For example, teachers are also expected to incorporate high levels of discussion and questioning techniques with their students. This may be one of the most consequential areas of instruction that ensures the highest levels of rigor and learning for students. However, mastering the intricacies of sound questioning techniques is not required on the first day of instruction. The novice teacher has the luxury of developing this skill set over a longer period of time without dire consequences for students.

Preservice teachers must recognize that there is a fundamental difference between what is important and what is urgent. Some teacher traits combine both. Some are important to varying degrees. The requirements to be an excellent teacher are diverse and interrelated, but each indicator is not equal to the others.

For example, most teacher evaluation rubrics will note the way in which teachers are connected to their school district and community. This is certainly an important consideration for a teacher. Becoming a part of the larger community is not optional and is critical if a teacher wants to educate her children holistically and understand the way in which educators can influence and understand the greater environment of which their classroom is one part.

However, developing this skill set cannot be a focus area before teachers develop sound practices in managing classroom procedures or develop strong instructional practices. New teachers should not only self-assess where their current skill levels are on the spectrum but should also note which areas of professional performance are most time-sensitive and bring particular focus to those areas in the beginning of their transition into the classroom.

In reviewing two of the most popular teacher evaluation systems, both articulate over twenty different areas of performance that must be defined and tracked. Keeping track of twenty distinct areas of performance is daunting. Considering that each discrete area is highly nuanced and complicated adds to the demand placed upon teachers. However, each of the areas is certainly important enough that it must be included. No one could suggest that paring the list down for the sake of efficiency would be helpful if it removed critical concepts such as communicating with families, setting learning objectives, or managing student behavior.

In reality, teaching is a highly complicated profession that is both science and art. While it may indeed seem overwhelming to attend to the wide variety of demands of the profession, a new teacher must embrace the reality that the profession is complicated and diverse by nature, and teachers must create a system for themselves to gauge, track, and grow in their performance of each area.

A critical mistake that preservice and new teachers make is to wait for a formal evaluator to weigh in on each aspect of their performance. When a teacher waits for another to initiate the first conversations about the critical aspects of the job and how a teacher is progressing, that teacher is failing to own his own professional growth and development.

It is no wonder that teachers feel dread and anxiety when they receive their performance evaluations. These conversations could be completely transformed if new teachers were committed to holding themselves to the high standards of the evaluation rubric on a daily basis. If teachers honestly reflect in these ways, gathering genuine evidence throughout their teaching experience, there will be a constant understanding of areas of strength and needed areas of focus at all times.

As with most recommendations, engaging in these practices is entirely optional. Most teachers will not be conscientious enough to track their own performance in these ways. These practices will undoubtedly add a lot of work upon already busy and overwhelmed preservice teachers. Because of that, many will forgo the recommendations and shift into survival mode. However, engaging in the optional work that others refuse to do is always what makes the difference in quality of preparation. The entire profession of teaching is marked with opportunities that are essential but not necessarily required.

It is in doing things that are optional that a beginning teacher sets herself apart from others. Prospective teachers will have to compete for a job and strong preparatory work will not go unnoticed by schools looking for the best teachers. While certain colleges may have more robust preparation programs for teachers, they are all likely to cover the same basic material and have similar requirements. This creates a situation where all candidates will likely look very much the same to an outsider making employment decisions.

Further, prospective teachers must recognize that inherent personality traits and characteristics may not emerge to a large degree in an interview setting.

Typical interviews settings are a series of questions that are asked by a team and answered by the candidate. Some aspects of a candidate's personality may emerge, but it is also within the highly structured interview setting and that may not be conducive to revealing the truth of who the teacher really is.

The difference between candidates is largely determined by the experiences that each candidate can draw upon and articulate to others. By definition, new teachers will have very little experience in quantity and must rely upon the quality of their limited experience to demonstrate their preparation and value. Being mindful of the need to be competitive serves as a powerful motivation as preservice teachers make decisions on the extra efforts they are willing to pursue during their teaching experience.

The work of preservice teachers is to become something more than they currently are. In becoming more than what they are, they able to set themselves apart from peers who are also trying to do the same. As much as people have in common, everyone is also incredibly different. In fact, people like to express their admiration for others by describing how special someone is. However, many have misunderstood what it means to say that someone is special.

For many who have been told that they are special, there is a mistaken belief that they are somehow better or privileged over others. It is easy for people to believe that they are special in a way that puts them in a position of entitlement over those around them. No one is special in this way.

People are indeed special, but in the respect that everyone is unique. This is no less noteworthy. But, instead of believing some are better than others, teachers should instead recognize that everyone's unique attributes have a special purpose. Everyone is a unique combination of blessings, talents, and skills. The task for teachers is to use those gifts in a way that maximizes their individual potential as they serve those around them.

Moreover, it is the teachers' duty to build and strengthen the innate gifts that have been given to them through discipline, practice, and study. When uniqueness is viewed in this way, people are indeed special.

As a teacher begins reimagining what preparing for this career should look like, this fact is important to consider. Teachers must strive to become special by developing their uniqueness. A teacher is like a key that fits a lock. Knowing that the cut of the key makes a person perfectly designed and equipped for specific purposes that others may not be able to fulfill is something that should instill a moral commitment to be as helpful and useful as possible.

Teachers should strive to become a master key. Some keys open one lock, but a master key is cut in a way that it can open many locks. Teachers must strive to build attitudes, dispositions, and skills that cut their key in a way that makes them able to be a master key to as many children as possible.

This approach acknowledges that people are indeed special but not in the sort of way that diminishes the special attributes of everyone around them. They too are keys; they too have locks that they are uniquely designed to open. Viewing others in this way also stresses the fact that everyone has similar but distinct purposes in this world.

In many ways, the work that lays ahead is an attempt to identify and then sharpen these traits that will best serve others. It is in this way that teachers can truly live a life full of great purpose and consequence for those who need the most assistance.

Who are you becoming? This question is at the heart of the professional development of the novice teacher. What began as an exercise in self-assessing present levels of performance invariably leads teachers to a place where one must design their own professional brand name.

In the same way that commercial brands speak to a consumer, so too does the professional brand that a person embraces. Does the average shopper throw any old brand of coffee into the shopping cart? People have strong brand loyalties for certain products.

Sometimes it is not clear whether the brand has true value or only if the prestige of the brand implies a value. Regardless, marketers and advertisers spend a small fortune convincing the public about their products. The marketers are not just trying to relay information that their product exists. Rather, they are trying to make the consumer believe and feel that certain qualities exist that transcend the product. Indeed, people have both strong intellectual and emotional reactions to the products in their lives: Walt Disney, Coca-Cola, Ford Motors. These products not only conjure images of what these companies represent but constantly remind consumers that they provide the very thing that their competitors cannot.

What is your brand name? If coffee drinkers are supposed to feel strongly about their favored brand, what should students and parents feel about your brand? Preservice teachers should spend some time reflecting on what they desire their brand name to communicate: hard working? caring? dedicated? Teachers should consider which attributes they believe they possess and find ways to build their skills and capitalize on these qualities. Moreover, teachers should examine which qualities they may not currently possess but intend to develop.

In the following scenario, a mentor is trying to get her new preservice teacher, Kelly, to consider the idea of what a brand name might possibly mean for her as she transitions into the profession:

Mentor: Thanks for coming today. Your advisor said you might be stopping by.

Kelly: I am so happy that you were willing to meet me. My name is Kelly.

Mentor: It's nice to meet you, Ms. Rogers.

Kelly: You can certainly call me Kelly.

Mentor: I appreciate that, but I think we should talk more about Ms. Rogers than Kelly.

Kelly: I'm not sure I follow you.

Mentor: Let's back up a bit and I'll show you what I mean. Tell me a bit about yourself.

Kelly: Well, I grew up in Texas and attended college there. I spent some time overseas studying abroad. I just moved here a few months ago. What else? I have a younger brother back in Texas and enjoy hiking and the outdoors. Is that what you mean?

Mentor: Kelly sounds like a wonderful person. Kelly is the person who brought you to this very place and you should be very proud to be Kelly. But who is Ms. Rogers?

Kelly: Hmm. I guess I haven't really thought of the difference. I must admit it is kind of weird to hear you call me that.

Mentor: You have been Kelly for a long time. It means something to you and it should. However, I need you to begin thinking about who Ms. Rogers is.

Kelly: Well, I guess I have a picture in my head of how I hope teaching goes.

Mentor: That's a good start. You are entering a whole new world. *Who* do you want Ms. Rogers to be?

Kelly: I'd like my students to like and respect me. I want them to know I care about them and their success.

Mentor: Now we are starting to get somewhere. Think of it this way. You will have a young boy named Gerald in your class. He struggles a bit in school. When he goes home after the first day that you're here, how do you want him to describe his new teacher to his parents?

Kelly: I want him to say that he has a new teacher and she was warm and friendly. I want him to say that she thinks I can learn a lot and she is going to help me do well in school.

Mentor: Yes. That is Ms. Rogers. It may be Kelly too, incidentally. But Gerald will only know Ms. Rogers. Ms. Rogers will be whomever you show him to be.

Kelly: I like that.

Mentor: And let me tell you, Gerald's parents worry greatly about him. You need to inspire their confidence that their beloved son is in good hands. They have no interest in placing their son in the care of Kelly. They will not have faith in Kelly, but I do believe they will have total confidence in Ms. Rogers. They need to see an adult caring for their son, not a student.

Kelly: Yeah, I never thought of how the parents will view me. I need to think more about that.

Mentor: Oh, one last thing. They will never know Ms. Rogers to be the person you tell them you are. They will only know you by what you show them. Show; don't tell.

The mentor imparts several important ideas to Ms. Rogers in this scenario. To begin with, the mentor acknowledges that Ms. Rogers has a strong primary discourse. Up to this point, it has been the way in which she has described herself to strangers and is the person she really believes she is.

However, the mentor also is quick to remind her that this may be the foundation for how she presents herself in the classroom, but it will not be the way in which the children know her. While she may share some of her back story as a way to make introductions, the students will soon set aside the biography of Kelly and begin doing business with Ms. Rogers.

This is especially true in building confidence in parent-teacher relationships. Parents are likely to have far less patience in allowing student teachers to learn their craft by trial and error using their children as test subjects. Parents will not expect perfection and can abide mistakes. However, they will only do so if they believe a professional made the mistake rather than someone who still views herself as someone not quite grown up.

The mentor also reveals the important lesson that the person students will know her to be will bear very little resemblance to the words she uses to describe the qualities she believes she has. A person does not believe another to be courteous because they say they are. A person believes another to be courteous because they show up on time and apologize when they make a mistake.

Preservice teachers need to begin by deciding which qualities they most want their students to know and believe about them. This is building the brand name. Ms. Rogers, Inc. This brand name speaks to people and embodies important and endearing qualities. Once preservice teachers embrace the qualities that they wish to represent, they must commit to growing and revealing those qualities in every encounter with other people.

Students coming out of college preparatory programs often are required to create a beliefs matrix that captures the tenets of the teaching profession that they value and the traits they believe are associated with them.

For example, they may have a section of their beliefs matrix that discusses classroom management. Under this header, there may be bullet points highlighting qualities such as: fair, firm, respectful, high expectations. A young teacher may certainly have to complete a matrix such as this for a course assignment but needs to reflect on how it ought to be used in practice. No one will believe teachers are respectful of others because their beliefs matrix declares that they are.

If a matrix like this is used to help a teacher keep track of important concepts in how they approach different aspects of their work, it may indeed serve a purpose. However, creating a bulleted list of adjectives will rarely convince anyone that teachers actually possess those qualities.

If teachers use a list of this sort to self-reflect on the brand name they are trying to build, it may be a very valuable tool. However, a list of characteristics describing a teacher's brand is only useful if the teacher then creates moment of human interaction with others where those qualities are lived. Brands are not declared; they are built.

Chapter 3

Reinventing Yourself

The most powerful kind of learning happens when a student embraces the work in front of him by adopting a teachable spirit. A teachable spirit is one that desires to know and understand and is willing to set aside preconceived notions of the way things ought to be done.

Having a teachable spirit demands great humility and a willingness to be stretched in ways that challenge fundamental beliefs and attitudes. Teachers try to instill this teachable spirit in their students and become frustrated when learners play defense against their attempts to help them grow in the classroom.

Adults must understand that the role of a learner is not exclusive to the young. The best teachers put themselves willingly into the role of a learner at every opportunity trying to squeeze more out of themselves with each passing day. There is a story about the famed and highly accomplished cellist, Pablo Casals, being interviewed about his intense practice routines, which lasted four to five hours per day when he was beyond eighty years of age. When asked why he still practiced so much, he responded by saying that it was because he believed he was really making progress.

Pablo Casals recognized that a teachable spirit is one that adopts a disposition toward learning at all times. Better than anyone, a teacher must recognize that this core attitude is essential. Preservice teachers must remain constantly open and positive to the thousands of learning opportunities that will present themselves each day.

As a young teacher reviews the self-assessment that defines her starting point as a teacher, she will have a brief window of opportunity to make sure that she approaches the work with the proper attitude and spirit to make her time in the classroom as productive as possible.

Many people are reluctant to allow themselves to approach new work with a teachable spirit. There are a few reasons why this may be. At times, people overestimate their own abilities and approach their assignment with a belief that they are already very accomplished and capable of doing the work.

While having a positive attitude and self-confidence are surely important qualities for teachers, they must be very careful in how they approach their student teaching assignment. It is very rare for anyone to be able to show great proficiency in skills that they have not practiced very much. A theoretical understanding of the tasks that need to be accomplished is very different than being able to perform these skills deftly in the moment with students.

On some occasions, people are not willing to adopt a teachable spirit because they are self-conscious of their lack of abilities. At one time or another, everyone has been faced with a situation where they feel as if they were an impostor. They were performing a task and were quite certain that someone would soon enter the room and let everyone else in on the secret that they were, in fact, completely incapable and unqualified to do the work that had been entrusted to them.

Novice teachers can silence the accuser whispering in the ear suggesting they are an imposter by remembering that everyone struggles at a task before they are proficient at it. If a person were handed an accordion and asked to play, most people would have no idea where to begin. Hardly anyone would feel bad about this fact. Instead, they would likely note that they had never played it before and had no idea where to begin.

However, sensible people seem to react in a completely different and irrational way when someone asks them if they can complete an equally foreign task that they wish they had mastered. The same person who has no shame in weak accordion skills may be quite embarrassed that they do not possess mastery in keeping a classroom full of teenagers under control and well managed. The novice teacher may have had no experiences with either challenge, but somehow feels bad about having weak classroom management skills even though she has never before attempted or practiced that skill.

Novice teachers must confidently acknowledge the skills they have attempted before and those they have not. Further, they must admit that they will likely struggle greatly in the beginning with all instructional demands and especially so with the areas they have never attempted.

However, with each admission they should simply say to their mentor, "I have never yet attempted that but look forward to doing so. I am sure I will struggle in many ways and look forward to any feedback and advice you could give me to help me get better. I can't promise you that I will instantly be good, but I do promise you that I will get better each day. I want to thank you in advance for your patience with me and allowing me to work on my skills."

When a teacher approaches the work in this manner, he can be sure that he is approaching the work with a teachable spirit. Some skills may come easily while others may be a constant struggle. Persisting in the work is the key.

Of course, every person is a mix of both strong and weak qualities and those personality traits can easily follow into the classroom. However, young teachers need to remember that, as they begin their preservice teaching experience, no one knows very much about them yet. This fact is a terrific advantage for the student teacher.

As novice teachers consider the brand name they intend to build for themselves, they start with a clean slate in their interactions with others. While teachers need to realize that they will have to demonstrate all of their positive qualities in every personal encounter, they should also recognize that they do not have to demonstrate any of their historical negative traits at all.

This is not to suggest that preservice teachers should be deceptive and hide their negative personality traits. Rather, it is the liberating notion that people are not compelled to act in ways that they have previously.

Suppose a young man grew up with a reputation for being lazy. This reputation was well earned through childhood. He was the kid who tried to sneak out of doing chores. He slept late and failed to keep his bedroom and possessions clean and tidy. Undoubtedly, his parents had to stay on him daily to attend to the most basic tasks.

Perhaps his laziness even extended to his studies. The young man turned in assignments late and lacked attention to detail as the work was usually done in a sloppy manner. Barely meeting expectations after being repeatedly hounded to get things done was standard operating procedure.

This unflattering portrait of a young man probably is a fitting description for more than a few people in this world. While not every hardworking person began his life in that way, the best employees were not necessarily industrious as children. Some people shed off their old habits and adopt new practices that leave their former ways behind.

If this young person were pursuing a career in education, he must come to a cross roads. The job expectations of a modern teacher leave little room for the lazy. This teacher has a decision to make. Either he will hold on to his poor work ethic and face a moment of truth with his principal where he is relieved of his teaching position for neglect of duty, or he will rise to the occasion. There has never been a job interview where the candidate secured the position by defending laziness.

At the moment where the lazy young man makes his transition into the profession, he could instead decide that the work entrusted in his care was important enough that he intends to turn over a new leaf. Those who hired him do not need to know he had to be forced to take out the trash as a kid. As long as he recommits himself going forward, he can shed his former bad habits.

This transition point from a student to a teacher is an optimal time to do just that. Some need to hit rock bottom before making needed changes in their lives. However, some make a fundamental change in their lives because the stakes have become significantly higher and it is now worth it to take a different approach.

Young teachers need to have this moment of truth with themselves before they make their first introductions in their student teaching assignment. Everyone they will meet will likely give student teachers the benefit of the doubt until they prove otherwise. This critical moment is the time for preservice teachers to guard against falling into their former habits and refrain from portraying any of their weaknesses to others. Those who are easily frustrated need to commit to patience. Those who are prone to anger must watch their temper.

The educational environment is a workplace. Employees do not have the luxury of freely expressing themselves in many ways. When people are on the job, they must maintain emotional control at all times. While reasonable people would recognize that this means that employees cannot misbehave in the workplace, responsible young teachers should take care that they also guard against revealing their personality flaws that could taint their experience and leave their mentors with few positive things to say in a future letter of recommendation.

This practice is not an act of deception. The young person is simply choosing to retire a bad habit within the professional work environment. If the young person in the scenario above chooses to continue to be a lazy person when he goes back home, that is certainly his prerogative. The commitment he is making is to his profession. Perhaps he is willing to tell his coworkers that he behaves in a completely different way outside of the work setting.

However, the message he is sending is that in this environment, he does not possess those traits. This young teacher is taking advantage of the tendency for good-hearted educators to extend the benefit of the doubt and presume positive intentions in those around them. Certainly, not everyone approaches others in this way, but those willing to open their classrooms as a mentor are likely to believe the best in others.

This is a characteristic that preservice teachers should adopt themselves from the very beginning. If others are going to presume the best about them, they should return that gesture. This means that everyone they encounter should be met with a positive and optimistic belief about their abilities and intentions.

If the preservice teacher is greeted by a grumpy mentor, he should assume nothing more than the mentor must be having a rough day and it is not representative of her true nature or personality. By refraining from judging others as they begin their work in the school environment, preservice teachers are more likely to be given a break by others when their certain shortcomings are revealed in the errors they make as they begin the complex requirements and tasks of being a teacher.

In all aspects of life, people should avoid falling into the trap of attribution bias. This is the psychological phenomenon where people often mistakenly attribute different motivating reasons for their own behavior than the reasons why others engage in the very same behavior.

For example, if a driver is cut off in traffic, it is easy for the driver to conclude that the other person is either a reckless driver or is very inconsiderate. However, if that driver were to do the same thing, he would often rationalize that he was forced to cut off the other person because he was in a hurry or simply made a slight mistake. When dealing with others, it is easy to fall into the trap that undesirable behaviors in others find their root in a flawed character.

Conversely, people seem to give themselves a bit more credit and attribute their behavior to unfortunate circumstances. As easy as this trap is to fall into, teachers of all levels of experience must guard against it. Teaching is a highly social activity, and the teacher will certainly be surrounded by others behaving at their very worst. Teaching children is too important and too delicate of a task to categorize others into good guys and bad guys.

That is not to say that conflict will not happen. Because education is a highly dynamic social environment, the complex social interactions that occur will undoubtedly give rise to periodic conflict.

Conflict with students is guaranteed. A teacher interacts with students daily in a variety of situations and is likely to ask them to complete tasks that they are not particularly interested in doing. Resolving the kind of conflict that arises with students should be part of a classroom management plan that is responsive to student behavior.

Conflict with other professionals in the building may be likely as well. Preservice teachers may wish to avoid all conflict of this variety and hope that it does not occur. Conflict is inevitable and arises between adults in a school setting for several reasons.

Some of the conflict that a young teacher may experience is not all negative. Many teachers are passionate about their profession and seek to engage in a lively debate, especially when others do not share their viewpoints. This is not necessarily a bad sign. While a novice teacher should be careful in how she engages in these sorts of debates, these conversations should not automatically be seen as a source or sign of dysfunction.

Even demanding veteran teachers can forgive a preservice teacher for not being a master teacher at the beginning. However, hardly anyone will forgive the novice teacher who approaches the practice or even conversations with an air of arrogance. This will likely alienate preservice teachers from peers even before they really begin the work.

This is most unfortunate because irritated veteran teachers may turn their attention upon proving the arrogant young teacher wrong rather than acknowledging the good work that is being done. In addition to the assigned mentor, other veteran teachers can provide assistance to the preservice teacher if they see the student teacher as a humble learner. Otherwise, they may only focus upon missteps that disprove the arrogant position the young teacher has taken.

If a young teacher approaches these difficult conversations in a polite and respectable manner, even tense conversations with others can yield powerful insights. Some teachers will offer unsolicited advice to the preservice teacher and may do so because they are very opinionated or simply because they desire to help. The student teacher should accept these comments with a positive outlook.

It is important to remember that offering an opinion in no way makes it true. Further, being offered advice does not compel the preservice teacher to act upon the advice. The one exception may be if the advice comes from the mentor teacher. In these situations, keeping an open and honest dialogue going with the mentor is essential to separate a suggestion from an expectation.

On other occasions, conflict may arise with colleagues because they are genuinely upset with something the preservice teacher has said or done. Assuming that the preservice teacher is not speaking inappropriately about others and is trying his best to meet expectations, the conflict should be resolvable. The conflicts are often rooted in misunderstandings or are based upon slights another person perceives.

Preservice teachers should seize the opportunity to meet with their peers and talk through the concern. Being direct in addressing problems has a dual effect. With those who are truly hurt by an action or comment, the preservice teacher will have an immediate opportunity to offer an apology or to clarify the true intent of his behavior. With those who desire reconciliation, this will send a powerful message of respect and a desire to address problems in a kind and professional manner. For those teachers who may feign that there is a problem, they too will be forced to address the problem in a direct and proactive way.

If teachers are voicing complaints simply trying to stir up some trouble, they will soon learn that it is easier to refrain from inventing imaginary problems because the preservice teacher will force them into a private and direct conversation. This is likely to be the sort of daylight that a troublemaker will seek to avoid.

Preservice teachers may also find conflict with others who simply are not very nice. Unfortunately, some educators do indeed seek to make others' lives more difficult. These people will often pick at another's sense of confidence by finding out which comments leave a young teacher vulnerable.

Trying to figure out why some people try to feel better about themselves by tearing others down is an exercise in frustration. Those types of people are all around and a few have likely worked their way on staff at schools too.

Preservice teachers should remain positive and confident despite these naysayers. If the problem is concrete enough to address, the young teacher should do so. Sunlight is the best disinfectant. Throwing light into all dark corners is often a remedy to get these people to turn their attention in another direction.

Aside from the required interactions, the preservice teacher should avoid unnecessary encounters with negative people. Regardless, the preservice teachers should address all worries about their performance with their mentor. If a negative partner teacher complains about a teacher's practice and the mentor dismisses the concern, the student teacher should not dwell upon it either.

The chief way for preservice teachers to avoid conflict is to ensure that they are *never* the source of it. As such, they should never put a critical voice to the things they hear and see other teachers doing. If the novice teacher feels compelled to inquire about something she has seen, she can certainly approach the mentor using the example in a hypothetical way. By attaching another person's name to inferior practices is a sure way to develop an irreparable reputation as a troublemaker.

Regardless of the source or type of conflict and criticism that novice teachers receive, they should not be quick to dismiss or make light of the concerns. Rather, they should reflect deeply on every piece of feedback they receive. If the criticism is untrue or unfair, the student teachers should cite specific examples of why it is not accurate.

For example, if a teacher across the hall makes a snide comment during lunch that the student teacher does not seem very prepared for the day's lesson, the student teacher should compile the evidence on her own behalf. *Did I prepare the lesson according to the expectation of my mentor? Is it as thorough and complete as my mentor's? Were there any occasions where my transitions seemed clunky and labored that may give the impression that I wasn't prepared?*

If the student teacher cannot find a fair basis for the comment, she should quickly dismiss it. However, the act of reflection (even on a mean-spirited comment) reinforces the student teacher's ability to reflect upon quality work and preparation. Even a negative comment meant to hurt ends up assisting the young teacher.

Conflict cannot be eliminated. It should be minimized and addressed when possible. When it cannot be addressed, it should be dismissed after careful reflection of any truth that may be contained in it. Whatever the source and intent, the preservice teacher controls how it will be processed and whether it will be turned to a greater good.

There is a great chance that young teachers will have their feelings hurt repeatedly as they begin their student teaching assignment. Novice teachers must remember that they are now adults functioning in a professional environment. They do not have to enjoy conflict, but they are obligated to deal with it in a productive and professional manner at all times.

Despite the inevitable difficulties that may arise in the work setting, preservice teachers must focus on maintaining a positive mental attitude throughout their experience. Teachers cannot always choose what other people will say and do in their interactions. However, everyone always has control of the way in which they will respond to an encounter.

Teachers should spend some time reflecting upon their own beliefs about others and the way they learn. Everybody's life is a work in progress. All people have strengths and weaknesses and those characteristics in action have an impact on everyone in the environment. Preservice teachers must recognize that the way in which other people behave may not always be pleasing but is usually the result of people acting in the best way they know how at that moment.

While people generally do the best they can, it is not to say that people cannot do better. Every professional in the field of education needs to do their job better. People do not always do better without the assistance of others. There is a name for those who help people learn a better way. These people are called teachers.

Teachers dedicate their lives to helping others learn. However, even teachers sometimes get caught in the fatalistic trap of forgetting that others are able to learn. Preservice teachers should begin by reflecting on their own personal beliefs about learning. People sometimes express negative beliefs about themselves and their own capacity to learn. *I've never been good at math. I'll never be able to speak in public.*

Preservice teachers should reflect on the narrative they tell about themselves. Whenever teachers state that they are incapable of learning and demonstrating skills, it sends a subconscious message that learning is not possible. This is in stark contrast to the very principle of teaching and learning. When teachers instruct their students, they learn. Certainly, some students take a bit longer than others and some require the instruction to take a different form than their peers.

The entire notion of education is predicated on the notion that learning at high levels is always possible. Preservice teachers should consider whether they sincerely believe this is true. Do teachers possess any negative beliefs about their own ability to learn? If they do suspect that learning is not always possible, do they take that errant belief into the way that they intend to interact with and instruct children?

Before falling into bad habits, preservice teachers must reframe the mindset that learning may not always happen. Failing to do so will not only severely limit the experiences that students have in their classes but will also affect the preservice teacher as she is trying to learn new skills throughout the student teaching experience.

If preservice teachers commit that they will learn how to teach at high levels, they are more likely to believe that their students are bound to learn at those high levels as well. When teachers commit to the belief that students will learn, their work then shifts into a problem-solving approach on how to reach a student who is struggling and will not get caught up in wondering if it is even possible for the child to learn.

Learning is serious business. Teaching children is a complicated affair full of depth and nuance that may escape the casual observer. Once preservice teachers commit to a mindset that unconditionally demands more from their own learning and that of their students, they must shift their focus to the rigors that will be required of them when they step into the classroom.

Preservice teachers must shift away from the student mentality that is seeking to meet minimum expectations and throw themselves headlong into the demands of the job. This commitment will require that student teachers arrive early to the school and plan to stay very late.

Mentor teachers will certainly notice the level of dedication that a preservice teacher brings to the job. Setting a tone of trying to get by in meeting expectations will not only fail to inspire confidence, but it will also likely result in a mentor teacher who is reluctant to invest completely back into the student teacher. Student teachers need to be able to access every possible opportunity that can be experienced on the job. Mentor teachers will not feel comfortable in taking any risks with a student teacher who seems to be clocking minimum hours.

This commitment requires that student teachers be willing to lend a hand in the preparation of the day's lessons. Some of this work will be mentally demanding in planning appropriate lessons in light of the student needs. Preservice teachers should also expect to spend time preparing the learning environment in other ways such as making copies and setting up lab equipment. Beginning teachers should not expect that some portions of the work will be set up for them by the mentor and they can then step into the day after much of it has been planned.

Likewise, there are several tasks that can be done only once students go home for the day. Teachers should plan to spend significant time cleaning up, grading papers, and preparing for the next day's lessons. Preservice teachers should work with their mentors stride for stride in every aspect of the job. Some may object and note that their mentor may not necessarily turn the grading of papers over to the student teacher right away. This may indeed be the case.

However, student teachers should insist upon making copies of all papers that need graded and ask their mentor if they can grade them in the evening to compare with the way in which the mentor has assessed them. Even though the mentor teacher's graded version will be the official one that gets handed back to the student, the student teacher has a terrific opportunity to practice assessing student work. The differences that can be found between the teacher's feedback to the students and the preservice teacher's feedback can be an incredibly enlightening experience.

Independent of the deep learning opportunity, it also sends a message to the mentor that the student teacher wants to join in the work rather than to observe the mentor doing all the work. This will make a strong impression from the beginning and will also help a student teacher develop a firsthand sense of the physicality and demanding nature of the profession. This cannot be experienced by watching.

Student teachers should also commit to attending every other function that their mentor attends. This includes faculty meetings, collaborative team meetings, school dances, district trainings, and family events. If a student teacher does not attend all aspects of the job, that teacher will never truly understand and appreciate the work. A true grasp of the complexity of the teaching experience comes from living all aspects of the profession as they intermingle with each other. Experiencing bits and pieces of the job in isolation fails to communicate the true complexity of the work.

Student teachers are already at a disadvantage in this regard as their assignments usually begin after the school year is under way. Because they arrive after the year has begun, student teachers miss a great deal of the reality of the classroom. For example, teachers expend a great investment of time and energy in the first few weeks of school, creating a positive experience for students. It is in this timeframe that the teacher learns about the students and quickly develops a working and caring relationship with them. The investment that a teacher makes in the affective domain with students in the first few encounters carries the relationship through the rest of the year.

It is also in this timeframe that a teacher establishes procedures and expectations that show students how they will find success in the classroom. The repetition and practice that goes into simple tasks that must be reinforced repeatedly is the way teachers establish a productive flow to the operation of their classroom.

Preservice teachers arrive on the scene after all the hard work is in place. Novice teachers must recognize that a substantial portion of the true work has been done for them and that they get the luxury of stepping into a setting that is usually running quite smoothly. Whichever portion of the year occurs in the absence of the preservice teacher arriving for the assignment is a gap and mystery that the preservice teacher must appreciate. Likewise, whatever skills they would have learned in these moments is a missed opportunity. The preservice teacher may not be able to backfill these skills. Getting classroom routines established happens only once in the school year. If the student teacher missed being a part of that process, she will have to do it for the first time during her first year of teaching.

The whole purpose of student teaching is to limit the number of experiences that preservice teachers will encounter for the first time during their first year of teaching. Spending some time with a mentor to hear the things that happened before the student teaching assignment began is a worthwhile investment. Which students were a challenge to get acclimated to the classroom environment? How do you teach procedures and expectations for the first time? These are the questions that a student teacher may have to hear about rather than experience firsthand. Forgetting that a substantial amount of work and preparation was invested in the classroom and children by the mentor is a colossal mistake.

As student teachers finish their preliminary preparations to enter the classroom and begin engaging with students in genuine acts of teaching, they should return again to the importance of coming into the work with a teachable spirit. Everything that is to come is going to be one of the greatest learning experiences of a lifetime packed into a few short months. The possibilities to grow and develop as a professional are countless in the living laboratory that is the classroom.

Student teachers should begin this transitional moment in a true spirit of appreciation. They have been given a gift. The gift is one that requires extra work and patience from many people to make the experience a success. The gift also includes sharing impressionable young students with the preservice teacher.

This gift should not be received lightly. Students will benefit greatly from the hard work and dedication of the student teacher. However, they will also feel the impact of any portion of the experience that does not go well. Preservice teachers should never forget that the children did not ask for a novice teacher to be their instructor. They deserve the very best education despite the fact that some portion of their education has been placed in inexperienced hands.

Student teachers should never forget this gift that has been given to them and should recognize that the best way to say thank you for this gift is to give their very best efforts at all times. Most of the mistakes that a novice teacher makes are reparable. However, failing to give the very best in every moment is simply inexcusable.

Chapter 4

Finding Your Voice

The work of the preservice teacher thus far has been centered on the necessary preparatory work before entering the classroom for the first time. Some of that work focuses on self-reflection of current skills, and other aspects of the work focuses on adjusting attitudes and beliefs to align with the demands of the job.

There are certainly expectations that school systems have for all preservice teachers and young teachers must determine how close their current habits and dispositions match those requirements. Student teachers must remain vigilant in monitoring how they are growing their capacity to close any gaps.

At this point in the student teaching experience, teachers must also find their own their own unique voice within the classroom. Preservice teachers can often vacillate between the extremes of being completely out of touch with the new expectations of functioning in a professional environment and feeling like they must squeeze themselves into a rigid mold that represents some notion of a "good teacher."

Preservice teachers must find their voice somewhere between these two extremes. Teachers must leave behind bad habits and work on their recognized weaknesses, but they also must capitalize on their unique personality in defining themselves as classroom teachers.

Students come in a wide variety of personality types, and the wide variety in teacher personalities adds a richness to classrooms. Having different voices leading the classrooms ensures that more students are served well.

Preservice teachers may assume that school leaders do not wish to see the individual characteristics of teachers emerge in the classroom. This could not be further from the truth. Although principals do not want to see negative attitudes and behaviors emerge within the classroom, the individuality of teachers does not need to be stripped away from classroom instruction either.

Student teachers should consider which aspects of their other "faces" may serve them well in the classroom. For example, a young teacher may recognize that her primary discourse in life to this point has been as a daughter and a student. These two faces have likely been the dominant roles where she has found an identity to this point in her life. She may also recognize that her emerging teacher face will now be an important role for her moving forward.

Because she has never been in the role of a teacher, however, she may be at a loss on what this teacher face should include. Suppose that she has built a strong reputation among her peer group in college as being highly conscientious and kind toward others. Obviously, this is a quality that would serve her and her students well in the classroom.

To suggest that her new discourse ought to be a completely different set of qualities is certainly not advisable. The teacher should indeed incorporate that quality into her classroom voice adapting it in an appropriate way. Being kind is always important. However, the way in which a college student shows kindness to a friend may be somewhat different than the way she should show kindness toward a young child.

Adapting all good personality characteristics to a classroom-appropriate voice is the task. However, the voice a teacher is trying to develop is more than just the sum of her positive personality traits. The voice a teacher develops is also a blend of attitudes, beliefs, and expectations for children.

How then does a teacher develop a personalized voice when that very voice will be the way in which she begins to interact with students on the first day she meets them? Teachers should put effort into developing this voice but should also recognize that their teacher voice is a work in progress. In the same way that a teacher will build a stronger skill set in assessing her students' learning, she will also mold and refine her voice as she grows as a teacher.

However, in the first weeks of the student teaching experiences, teachers will be highly impressionable and may search for voices to adopt as their own. If a student teacher forms a strong bond with her mentor, she will likely begin imitating the voice that she hears daily in the classroom. In many ways, this can be a good thing. If a teacher has been placed with a strong mentor, there are likely many aspects of the mentor's voice that may be worth adopting.

There are inherent dangers to this as well. As generous as mentor teachers are in opening up the opportunity for a student teacher to be in the classroom, mentor teachers are not perfect. Aside from extreme examples of misbehavior on the part of adults, it is quite difficult for a novice teacher to differentiate between qualities of their mentor that are effective when the preservice teacher has very little experience in recognizing best approaches in the classroom.

Student teachers should carefully evaluate the voice of their mentor and contemplate which aspects of their mentor are worth emulating. However, this should not be limited to qualities that are deemed admirable. Young teachers must also recognize that many traits of their mentor simply do not fit with their own personality.

For example, if a mentor teacher possesses an outgoing personality and interacts with students in a dynamic sort of way, students may likely enjoy and respond to the dynamic nature of the teacher. A student teacher may prize this quality and decide that it is a quality that should be incorporated into his own teaching voice. However, if the student teacher is quiet and reserved by nature, interacting with students using the same approach may not come across in the same way as his mentor.

In these cases, a student teacher's admiration of another may result in them becoming a cheap imitation of the mentor. While the quality is indeed admirable, it must be integrated into the personality of the student teacher in a genuine way lest she feel compelled to drive the personality square peg into a round hole.

Novice teachers will be presented with these possibilities countless times per day during their student teaching experience. Trying to decide which attitudes and behaviors to adopt and which ones to disregard can feel like a daunting task. To some degree, this is part of the complex task of learning to become a competent teacher. However, this could easily overwhelm a new teacher who is trying to do her best to make sensible decisions.

Student teachers can employ a technique to bring coherence with the myriad considerations and suggestions that are sure to be presented along the way. Student teachers need to engage in a reflective technique called *intentional decision making*. Intentional decision making is a deliberate effort to understand every decision that is made within the classroom setting.

In the beginning of the student teaching experience, mentor teachers will likely take a leading role in classroom instructional practices. Rather than assuming that the mentor teachers simply know best and accepting their practices outright, the student teacher needs to keep extensive notes on what is happening in the classroom.

Using three-column notes as a way to track thinking, the preservice teacher needs to record every action and decision that a teacher is making. Whatever actions, statements, questions, and dispositions that the teacher presents to students, the student teacher should record in the first column of the intentional decision-making chart.

The student teacher should then fill the second column of the chart with a hypothesis of why the teacher likely made that decision. Certainly, the student teacher may be wrong about why the teacher took the particular course of action but reflecting on the possible reason is a great learning opportunity. By considering why these decisions are being made, the novice teacher begins to understand that decisions that are made are of consequence in the classroom.

The preservice teacher must then capture a piece of time with the mentor teacher to discuss the occasions where there could be possible confusion or misunderstanding. The preservice teacher should then fill out the third column by visiting with the teacher to ascertain why the mentor did, in fact, make certain decisions. Again, reflecting on the differences that the student teacher assumed compared to the reasons that the mentor cites creates another powerful learning opportunity.

It is not enough to just fill in the third column, however. Student teachers should spend significant time discerning why they made their assumption and if that assumption was right or wrong. The ultimate goal should be to gain insight into the way in which teachers arrive at their decisions in a more accurate way. As the teacher gets better at this, they will be more equipped at seeing the opportunity to make good decisions themselves in their classroom.

Often, student teachers can make assumptions that are not exactly wrong but are not completely right. There can be both surface and deep reasons why people behave the way they do. Examples of this can be found in all walks of life.

In modern boxing, when a boxer stands up after being knocked down, fans will usually notice that the referee will grab the fighter by both wrists and rub the front of the boxer's gloves up and down the front of the referee's shirt. Seeing this routine is quite curious and is often a very odd action as an injured boxer is trying to collect himself. The reasons behind this action are quite informative to the observer who seeks to understand the intention of someone's actions.

In the early days of boxing, fighters wore boots into the ring that had leather soles on the bottom. Because the ring would get wet from the boxers' sweat and the water that was spilled in their corner between rounds, the ring would get very slick. As a solution, corner men would have a box of rosin in the corner for the fighter to step into to coat the soles of his boots. This would help to keep the boxer from slipping as he moved around the ring during the fight.

In the event that a boxer were to get knocked down, his gloves would often pick up some of this rosin as he helped himself to his feet. The referee would remove this rosin off of the gloves by wiping them on his own shirt. This prevented the coarse rosin from being a foreign object that could cut the other boxer or get in his eyes blinding him.

For this reason, wiping a boxer's gloves on the front of a referee's shirt makes a lot of sense. However, it is interesting to note that boxers have not stepped into rosin boxes for many decades, yet the referees continue with this practice.

In looking for an intentional reason why referees continue this practice, there are a few possibilities. Lovers of tradition may suggest that this is a holdover practice that endures out of nostalgia for days gone by. There might be something to this explanation. After all, boxers still call the fighting area a ring even though boxers have not fought within a ring shape for ages.

It could also be argued that there may be other small particulates that are on the ring floor that could have a similar effect to rosin and it remains a precautionary measure that still makes sense to continue to do. This too may be a decent reason to continue the practice.

Regardless of the truth behind the other two reasons, seasoned referees know that there is a more fundamental and intentional reason for continuing this practice. Referees engage in this move after an injured fighter has returned to his feet. By moving in close enough to the fighter to grab his wrists, the referee has a few seconds while wiping the gloves to look deeply into the eyes of the vulnerable fighter. In these few seconds, referees assess the condition of the boxer to decide whether to allow him to continue.

This example parallels some of the inaccurate assumptions student teachers may make about the work they begin observing in the classroom. In the following scenario, Mr. Jenkins has completed an observation of his mentor and captured the observation using the three-column intentional decision-making activity. He then discussed his thinking with his mentor:

Mr. Jenkins: I wondered if we could chat for a little bit about today's lesson? I took down some notes and wanted to clarify a few things that I noticed.

Mentor: Sure. I'll be happy to help. What questions do you have?

Mr. Jenkins: Well, when you were having a class discussion today, at one point I noticed that you called on Justin even though he did not have his hand raised. I saw that five other kids did have their hand raised and wondered why you chose Justin instead?

Mentor: That's interesting that you picked up on that. What was your theory on why I may have chosen to do this?

Mr. Jenkins: In my notes, I wondered if you felt like he was not paying close enough attention and asking him a question might make him more engaged in your lesson. Is that what was going on?

Mentor: I can see why you might make that assumption, but the truth of it is actually quite the opposite.

Mr. Jenkins: I am not sure I'm following you.

Mentor: Right now, Justin is on a losing streak in his academics. You are correct in noting that he has withdrawn and is a bit disengaged, but I did not ask him a question simply to put him on the spot. In fact, that could be a bit cruel considering everything he's dealing with in life right now. Instead, I disregarded those kids who had their hand raised simply because I knew that they had the correct answer. Calling on them does nothing more than confirm that certain kids always have the right answer. It would also confirm that everyone else's job to sit around and congratulate them for being right once again.

Mr. Jenkins: But how does calling on Justin solve that? Doesn't it take the chance that he will just get the question wrong and highlight the fact that he is struggling?

Mentor: That's a very insightful point. That tells me you're really thinking about this. Did you happen to notice the kind of question I saved for Justin?

Mr. Jenkins: I guess I did not really pick up on that in my notes.

Mentor: That's alright. The kind of question I asked him was very purposeful. I did not ask Justin a question that had one correct answer. If that were the case, there is indeed a good chance that he would have been wrong in front of his peers. But if you will remember, I asked him an open-ended question where he had an opportunity to give his opinion but asked that he back it up with some other evidence from the text. This nearly assured that the answer he gave would be in the ballpark of being correct.

Mr. Jenkins: Oh, yeah, I can see that.

Mentor: Also, I was quick to follow up with additional clarifying questions to pull the right answer out of him to patch up any parts of his original answer that were not fully correct.

Mr. Jenkins: Yeah, that makes sense.

Mentor: So, the outcome of that exchange was re-engaging Justin within our classroom conversation at the same time as we put him back on a winning streak. There is nothing more satisfying for a kid like him than to get to be right every now and then. Do you know how hard and frustrating school can seem if you never get to be correct? I created an opportunity today for Justin to finally have the right answer.

Mr. Jenkins: I'm not sure I would have thought of doing that myself.

Mentor: Don't be too hard on yourself. You are learning. If you had repeatedly watched Justin fall further and further into a losing streak, you would've created an opportunity just like I did. The task of the teacher is to figure out what needs to happen and create a possibility where it is likely to happen. That is all I did today.

The teacher in this scenario is obviously making all of the decisions in her class with great intentionality. She recognizes that simply verifying which kids have the correct answer is not the entirety of her responsibility as a teacher. Additionally, she values her role in assessing what each individual student most needs in that moment. While the other students who were raising their hands may have the desired validation in being correct, Justin's needs were more pressing in that moment and the teacher recognized it.

The student teacher did many things correct in his observation of the classroom. He obviously took detailed notes of what was going on in the classroom and chose to engage with the mentor when he could not make sense of what he observed. It was in embracing this active participation role as an observer that the student teacher was even able to engage in the kind of conversation that ultimately was very valuable to his growth as a teacher.

Without the student teacher taking this active role, the events of the day would have quietly passed by without further thought or reflection. This example would not have likely occurred to a mentor teacher to serve as a powerful instructional moment. These are the kind of decisions that expert teachers make countless times per day. Student teachers cannot hope that their busy mentor has the capacity to note and remember all of the important actions they are taking in each moment.

With this particular example, Mr. Jenkins misunderstood the actions of his mentor teacher. This should not come as a surprise. Many teacher decisions will not be understood upon first glance and will require further discussion to understand the intention behind the decision.

In the same way as a referee who does one thing with a deeper, underlying purpose, teachers often engage in one action that makes sense at some level to a casual observer. However, many important behaviors of the teacher are under the surface. The only way in which a novice teacher will ever understand this nuance is to ask focused questions.

When novice teachers hear that they should ask a lot of questions when they begin their student teaching experience, it is easy to internalize that message to mean that they should ask how to do things. How do you write a solid lesson plan? How do you decide how hard to grade a paper? Student teachers may certainly wonder at these kinds of questions and asking a mentor is certainly appropriate and helpful.

Although asking *how* is beneficial, the more informative question begins with *why*. The entire point of the intentional decision-making exercise is to ask *why* in a more structured way. However, even asking why can become stale and routine. That is why predicting why teachers act the way they do is so helpful.

Student teachers may feel vulnerable and self-conscious by asking too many questions. This fear should be immediately set aside. Good mentors recognize that everything is new to the student teacher and they will need to ask many questions as they experience everything for the very first time.

There is another reason why student teachers should embrace the habit of asking questions continually. Mentor teachers want good things for students. They recognize that students will benefit if student teachers are better prepared to enter the classroom. Every question student teachers ask decreases the chance that they will make those mistakes with children when they are teaching on their own. The patience that a mentor is required to show in answering a barrage of questions is always worth it for this reason.

Thus far in the student teaching experience, the preservice teacher is mostly observing the mentor teacher. As the intentional decision-making task demonstrated, observation is not a passive activity.

This is a mistake that preservice teachers can easily make. They assume that they are watching the mentor teacher when they should be making observations. There is a fundamental difference. Watching someone assumes a passive role. When watching someone, there is no obligation on the part of the watcher to do anything other than to follow another with the eyes.

Observing someone is quite different. Observing requires everything that watching does, but also requires the observer to pay attention in a more structured way. *What just happened? Who caused it? How did the others respond? Who reacted positively? Who reacted in a negative way? Who didn't react at all?*

Beyond the simple observations of who, what, where, when, and why, active observers must get deeper. *Why did it happen? What was the fallout of the decision? How has the environment now changed? Are things better or worse? How might it have been done better?*

The ultimate reason for student teachers to absorb information and learn in this way is to equip themselves to serve their students. Students deserve more than a teacher who clocks time and goes through the motions. Intentional decision making ensures that the right things are done for the right reasons.

More than ever, students need teachers to be excellent at what they do. Because students come into classrooms in a more fragile state and with far more complicated lives than ever before, teachers must be ready to create an environment to support them properly.

Long gone are the days when a teacher stood in front of the room and transmitted information to the learner. In fact, that approach was probably never very effective for any but a select few students. The teacher must not only know how to teach but be able to do so under extreme circumstances with young people who are not very well equipped to learn at times.

Preservice teachers have begun their work considering who they themselves are and which characteristics they must bring to the work to be viewed and treated as professionals. They then entered the school embracing a learning attitude and teachable spirit by asking questions and observing the work of the mentor closely.

The next step for student teachers is to examine the way in which they will interact with students. The preservice teacher has committed to acting like a professional, placing serious importance on creating a respectable brand name. Embracing important and positive qualities is good theoretically, but it does not address how those qualities will manifest in the presence of students.

If a teacher decides she wants to be known as a professional who is kind to all others around her, it does not really clarify what she will say and do in the presence of students to demonstrate that quality. Preservice teachers may hear others speak of the classroom environment. Evaluation instruments put great emphasis on the importance of maintaining an effective and positive classroom environment. The novice teacher may rightly ask what this actually means.

It is a mistake to view the classroom culture and climate as something that exists separate from the teacher in the room. The teacher sets the tone of the environment. The teacher controls what is allowed to happen in the environment. The teacher herself is the classroom environment.

When students walk into any room, they behave in the way that is acceptable. A student who has excellent behavior may act completely out of control in the school library if that is the prevailing culture. Likewise, a student who struggles with inappropriate behavior year after year may be a model student in a certain teacher's class. How is it that the same child behaves at complete opposite ends of the spectrum depending upon the room?

The answer is that it has far less to do with the student than the room. Of course, there is nothing magical about a classroom. Students do not alter their behavior because of the posters hanging on the wall or the arrangement of the chairs. The classroom environment is synonymous with the way in which the teacher treats others.

The preservice teacher may flinch at this and wonder if it also has something to do with the way in which the students treat each other. Certainly, it does. However, the way in which students treat each other has everything to do with the actions of the teacher.

Preservice teachers must acknowledge from the beginning that no work of significant consequence will happen in the classroom if students do not feel safe, secure, and empowered in the classroom. It matters little if the teacher is a content expert if students are not engaged in the instruction. It will not matter if a teacher pulls together exciting materials for the day's lesson if students do not feel valued and heard by their teacher and those around them.

Everything of consequence that is to follow depends upon the way in which the teacher consistently treats students and demands that they treat each other. While having the proper disposition is important, attaching an attitude to a concrete behavior is the way to make a positive culture come alive.

For example, suppose a teacher commits to the idea that she wants all students to know she is glad they are in her class. What things could she do that would show that? Certainly, one concrete behavior could be to commit to greet every student at the door each day with a high-five. Every day, students file past their teacher and she slaps their outstretched hand. But is that enough? Might it seem odd when done in isolation? She may also realize that it should be accompanied with a genuine greeting.

> Good morning!
> I'm glad you are here today.
> I missed you yesterday.

These are the kinds of statements that send a strong positive message to students about what to expect even before they step in the door. Students will likely leave behind some of their frustration and anxiety of the outside world by being greeted in such a way.

The student teacher should also consider what sort of body language is being communicated to students when being greeted at the door. Student teachers bring the normal stressors of life and the incredible stress of beginning the student teaching experience with them when they begin each day.

Students have an incredible knack for picking up on the affect of the adults around them. While adults often disregard this fact, children are incredibly good judges of character. Students know when an adult does not like them. Likewise, students also recognize genuine care and concern for their well-being. In fact, students will gravitate toward adults who care about them.

Well-intentioned teachers may wonder how to express their care for their students. Obviously, adults need to maintain appropriate boundary lines at all times with children. In fact, while students are good judges of their teacher's character, they do often seek to blur the boundaries that a teacher should maintain. This only makes sense. If a student is lacking an emotionally supportive adult in his life, he may be drawn to someone who does offer this support. Students do have a hard time distinguishing between a caring and emotionally intimate relationship, though.

This should not scare young teachers away from showing care for their students. Instead, they simply need to be mindful of that their care for their students should play out within the context of the classroom. When this is the case, teachers have nothing to fear by communicating their care for their students.

Besides greeting students at the door and offering them a fist bump or a high-five, a teacher can communicate the care behind their warm greeting by simply smiling at the students when they come through the door. This act seems entirely too simple, but it is often overlooked by harried teachers. Slowing down long enough to offer a smile to kids when they enter the room is often all it takes to transform the attitude of students.

Novice teachers usually embrace the idea of communicating warm and caring attitudes for their students but often overthink how that is best done. A teacher should not stand in front of the classroom and say, "I care about you kids." Students would likely be confused by such a contrived approach to building rapport with them. Instead, teachers should reflect upon the other relationships in their lives. Care for students is clearly communicated by smiling at someone and asking them how the things they find important are going for them.

Relationships matter. Relationships with students are not built by announcing the desire to get to know them. Relationships are built one smile and one pleasant conversation at a time. Students know they are liked and supported by their teacher in these informal moments. The good news is that there are plenty of opportunities to build these critical relationships. The bad news is that each opportunity is so subtle that it can quietly pass by if a teacher does not seize the moments to connect with students.

The heart of great teaching is being responsive to what each student needs in that moment. Educators put a great deal of thought into the academic needs that students have and build complex systems of support around students who are struggling. These practices are certainly important, but they are premature at this time for the novice teacher.

From the beginning of the student teaching experience, preservice teachers must build strong foundations to support the academic learning that needs to happen in their class. Students cannot be expected to operate at levels of academic performance if more basic needs are unmet. For some, this literally means food, shelter, and safety. For these students, teachers must bring together support personnel to wrap resources around the child.

Most students, however, have those basic needs met and are struggling to find necessary security that comes with finding a place of belonging in an environment that can sometimes be quite stressful. The public school classroom is a place where students who may not know each other very well must come together to acknowledge what they do not know in order to learn important skills.

This requires a level of risk taking that demands incredible confidence. Because educators themselves often enjoyed school and had a pleasant experience, they can easily forget that the same security is not always an automatic reaction for many students. However, teachers can create the supportive and caring environment where all of this work is possible.

This environment is not created automatically and is in danger of being disrupted or destroyed with every stray comment or negative behavior that is not addressed within the classroom. A healthy classroom environment is very fragile. Student teachers must recognize that this is their most fundamental task. It is from this place that everything of consequence will happen.

Student teachers can formalize this process by assessing the culture and climate of their classroom each day. In the same way that teachers are asked to track the academic progress of their students, novice teachers must systematically record and track the lived experience of all of their students each day. Who seemed to thrive today? Who was withdrawn? Who acted out of character? Why might this be?

Preservice teachers are too new to managing a classroom to leave the status of their classroom culture to chance. Like delicate flowers in the garden, the experience of students in the classroom must be carefully tended each day. Despite those who suppose outside factors in students' lives dictate the inevitable tone of the classroom, master teachers know that their classroom is the one bit of the world within their control.

The classroom belongs to the teacher. The teacher can choose to reflect positivity and joy in all that they do. The teacher can choose to treat students well even when the student is not showing mutual respect. The teacher can choose to teach kindness and gratefulness in every interaction with students. Teachers should embrace the fact that their classroom may be the one bit of respite for young people in their lives. The classroom can be the one place in the world where goodness, fairness, and kindness always win. To gloss over this powerful reality is to miss the entire point of being a teacher.

Chapter 5

Learn Your Craft (or Find Another)

The old man looked closely at his young apprentice covered in saw dust leaning over the workbench. "Son, the boards you just cut were neither square nor the right length."

The young man let out an exasperated sigh, saying, "I did the best I could. Isn't it good enough?"

"No, it is not good enough. In fact, it isn't even good let alone good enough. We are craftsmen. We are called to greater things than cutting lumber although that skill is certainly a necessary first step."

The old man picked up another board and looked the young apprentice in the eye. He said, "Son, you must learn your craft or find another."

Just like the combined skills of artistry required of the master wood worker, teaching is a craft. Teaching requires the combination of a highly creative art form with a highly disciplined scientific technique. To become a great teacher requires the mastery of both the art and science of teaching.

Becoming a master at anything requires attention to the technique of the discipline and focused practice at the component elements. Because teaching is a highly social activity focused on unpredictable children, many forget that there is a wide base of professional research that describes the kinds of activities and approaches that assist students in their learning and others that do not.

The instructional approaches that work the best with students are clearly defined and readily available to any teacher who wishes to use only the practices that have been proven to work. A novice teacher may rightly wonder why they see such variability in the practices that are observed in the classroom.

The reality of many classrooms is that teachers often engage in approaches that do not work. For example, many student teachers may still witness teachers using a strategy called round-robin reading. This method of oral reading is characterized by students reading a passage of text of a predetermined length while other students follow along. When the reader completes a portion of the passage, the next student picks up where that student left off and takes her turn. This approach has been used for hundreds of years by countless numbers of teachers. The problem is that it does not work.

Because professional researchers have taken a keen interest in studying and promoting the tactics that assist student learning, educators do not have to guess whether an approach is effective. Repeated studies have shown that round-robin reading has three negative effects on readers.

First, it stigmatizes weak readers. Most people can remember being a part of a round-robin reading group as a child and watching a classmate disconnect from the class as he read ahead and mentally rehearsed his paragraph that was coming up to avoid the pending embarrassment that was soon to follow. If the purpose of this style of reading is to aid in comprehension, struggling readers learn nothing more than their weaknesses as readers are on public display for all to witness.

Also, when students listen to their peers orally and they are reading too fast or too slowly, or if their reading is haltingly interrupted by errors, they become distracted to the point where their overall comprehension is weakened. This is the exact opposite of the desired effect a teacher is seeking when practicing reading.

Although oral reading does increase fluency in students, this works only when good reading is modeled. When struggling readers model poor fluency or mispronounce words, weak fluency becomes the model. This compromises the very fluency oral reading seeks to strengthen.

Why then do teachers continue these weak practices? Student teachers must recall the temptation to model their teaching after their own teachers when growing up. Their own teachers may have implemented poor practices and they have been passed down to subsequent generations.

This is completely unnecessary. Poor practices can be eliminated immediately when teachers make commitments to using only the best techniques that have been proven to work. Because school leaders rarely see or intervene regarding classroom choices, some of these weak practices are perpetuated.

Student teachers have not yet acquired bad habits in their instructional choices and must commit from the very beginning to learn the techniques of their trade. Quite simply, student teachers do not yet have jobs. They do not have the luxury of employing any weak practices or cutting any instructional corners.

Preservice teachers are entering a sixteen-week interview process. While that can seem rather daunting, it comes at the advantage of being able to learn, experiment, regroup, and reapply method after method to refine their craft. However, before beginning on the first day, preservice teachers should begin their own studies of effective classroom instruction. By internalizing those instructional practices that have positive effects, they can start building their own skill set. Teachers will invariably make mistakes, but they must employ focused and sensible trial and error.

If the professional literature supports the proper implementation of a strategy, teachers should embrace it by learning more. What is the strategy? How is it implemented for a particular age group? When is it effective? When might it not be effective? This is the level of professional thoughtfulness that must be considered by even new teachers.

The thought of testing out proven instructional practices with a group of young people can seem quite stressful. Indeed, the student teaching experience is quite stressful. However, stress should not be seen as an automatically negative state of being. Everyone has experienced both healthy and destructive types of stress in their lives.

Healthy stress challenges and stretches the person in important work to expand a level of competence that is not acquired automatically. Healthy stress is high stakes but is working through a productive channel and is translating into results.

Destructive stress is quite different. This sort of stress is borne out of frustration and repeated failure with no hope of turning it to a greater good. This stress is fueled by negativity and pessimism. This stress should not be emblematic of the student teaching experience.

Preservice teachers must find a comfort level within the healthy stress of a teaching environment. Certainly, there will be moments of frustration and perceived failure. However, embracing a growth mindset that every failed attempt is a lesson learned that will never need to be repeated is the way to work through difficult times with a spirit of hope and optimism.

A fundamental truth that can never escape the mind of the student teacher is this: results matter. They are not called to run out the clock of their student teaching experience; they are called to ensure that students grow as learners during this time. Student teachers should not expect that their time is spent experimenting with the new set of skills they have acquired during their college experiences. Rather, they are called to utilize those skills and put them to immediate use to assist students in their learning.

Results are not for another day; results are expected immediately. Results cannot wait until the mentor teacher resumes control of the classroom. Instead, student teachers must expect to see daily growth in their students even while they are still learning their craft.

Just as commercial travelers expect proficiency from their pilot on their very first solo flight, so too must student teachers expect competency from themselves from the very beginning of their time in front of kids. This is not too much to expect. Preservice teachers have every opportunity to build their own skill set independent from the guidance of their mentor to ensure that they meet this expectation.

The first lesson for the student teacher in this regard is that there is no place for inferior teaching practices in the classroom. There is no mystery. Researched-based best practices are widely known and available. Student teachers must crack the books and dive into the results of decades of educational research and begin with the practices that will help students while refusing to utilize the methods that do not work.

You cannot teach what you don't know. Teachers must examine the component pieces of teaching and learning and make sure that they have a thorough understanding of the work they should be doing independent of whether they are very good at doing those things.

Preservice teachers must begin their understanding of their work by grounding their learning in the content standards for their grade and discipline. Despite the opinion that standards are densely packed ideas nearly impenetrable to the average reader, there is a wealth of information hidden in each if one takes the time to unpack them properly.

This is certainly worth the trouble as teaching the adopted state standards is the fundamental task of the teacher. While teachers must never lose sight of the students who will be learning them, teachers cannot underestimate the importance of having a strong grasp of the demands that the standards require.

For example, suppose a standard were to require a student to do the following:

> Analyze specific textual evidence to support an argument in a text noting important biases the author has and any inconsistencies in the account.

An inexperienced teacher may become quite overwhelmed reading standards like this, noting their sheer complexity and number. However, teachers must systematically break these standards down to determine what they must ask their students to do. In looking at the verbs in the sentence, students are required to "analyze." This is an easy and important first step for a teacher to consider. The students are not being asked to compare two things. They are not being asked to discuss a topic. Students are being asked to analyze something. What is the something the students must analyze? Of course, the standard reveals the answer. They must use a text to analyze evidence within that text.

The task of the teacher becomes clearer as each component of the standard is teased apart. Students need to use a text to find evidence. Now, the teacher must look deeper. What kind of evidence must the student find? The standard reveals that they will be searching for evidence the author cites to support an argument.

If the standard is not asking the student to list or discuss the arguments that the author makes, what exactly is the student analyzing? The student is analyzing the biases and inconsistencies that the author may put forward in making the argument.

At this point, the preservice teacher can begin formulating a bit of a plan on what to do next. Obviously, the teacher needs to put a text in front of the students. Which sort of text is most useful for this task? A novel would be senseless as the standard is demanding that the students work with a text where the author makes an argument. The teacher may imagine an opinion piece in a magazine where the author makes bold claims and tries to substantiate the argument.

This kind of text would set students up for success. The teacher would indeed need an article that makes an argument. At this point, is the teacher ready to make some copies and set the students loose to complete an assignment that reflects the demands of the standard?

The novice teacher must remember the important lesson that should always be at the center of their instruction: A teacher can never ask a student to do something that they have never been taught to do. Has the teacher taught the students how to analyze a piece of text?

There is a technique to everything and conducting an analysis of a piece of text is no exception. To properly analyze a text, students must do a number of things. First, they must read the text thoroughly to understand the point the author is trying to make. Second, students must clearly write out a statement summarizing the argument the author is making. Third, students must list the reasons that the author gives in support of the argument. Next, students must consider which pieces of evidence seem to have valid counterarguments on the other side. Ultimately, students must discern which of the arguments do not seem to be logically sound due to the author's one-sided presentation of the argument. The discussion of this step is the final analysis that the standard demands.

Teachers must explicitly teach these steps if they expect students to apply them when conducting a literary analysis. Without this explicit instruction, teachers will likely demand that students complete a task without explaining how it is actually done. It is not unlikely to hear teachers say, "Produce an analysis of the text by analyzing it."

Student teachers must understand that students will likely attempt to complete assignments that they understand. However, telling them what to do and teaching them are not the same thing.

This exercise in pulling apart a standard demonstrates several things that teachers must do. It demands that they understand what students must know and be able to do. It also clarifies the cognitive depth at which students must do the task (analyze vs. summarize). Likewise, it also starts to clarify the kinds of materials the teacher must gather and the background skills the teacher must teach and review with the students.

Understanding how to break apart standards into student-friendly language is at the heart of designing appropriate and coherent instruction. Student teachers must also consult the adopted curriculum for their school at this point as well.

Preservice teachers must immediately distinguish between curriculum documents and instructional materials. A curriculum document lists the standards that are the focus of a unit of students and the pacing that the teacher should follow. Likewise, curriculum documents may list the essential questions or the enduring understandings that students should acquire over the course of study.

Curriculum documents may also present the appropriate vocabulary words that must be taught in order for students to understand the content of the unit of study. Often, these documents will also list the discrete items that students should both know and be able to know by the end of the unit.

Novice teachers should note that curriculum documents may also discuss the suggested materials that a teacher should use during this unit of instruction. However, teachers must firmly accept that teaching materials are not synonymous with curriculum documents. Teaching materials are the tools that teachers use to help students master standards.

The completion of a workbook page can never be the point of a lesson. Indeed, the teacher may use the workbook page to practice a component of one of the standards for the course, but the mastery of the standard is the goal. This can be an incredibly hard lesson for a teacher to embrace.

Novice teachers can often view instructional materials as a crutch to help them fill time in a way that feels appropriate for the course. Of course, teachers should not abandon their adopted materials. Rather, they should see them as the tools that they are and make conscious decisions not to over-rely on them.

The best way in which teachers can ensure that they are staying true to a standards-focused instructional approach is to break off a piece of a standard each day as the focus of the day's instruction. Further, teachers should post the portion of the standard on the board and the first portion of the day's instruction should be the creation of a learning target for students.

Learning targets are nothing more complicated than the portion of the standard that is being attempted in that class period rewritten in student-friendly language. Once the learning target for the day is established, students will know exactly what they will be doing during the class period and will know why they are doing it. This gives both the reason for the lesson and a sense of the relevance of how it fits into the bigger picture of their learning.

After teachers understand their own standards, how those standards fit into the curriculum documents for the unit, which materials to choose to meet them, and create learning targets for their students, the real work of instruction can begin.

At this point, a student teacher can certainly make mistakes in unpacking the standard that needs taught, but there really has not been any decisions to make. Despite the protests of some teachers, it has never been up to the teacher to decide what should be taught in the classroom. The guidance is completely clear in that regard and it is the adopted state content standards.

However, *how* a teacher should best approaches teaching the standards is certainly within her control. It is in these instructional choices that teachers must make countless decisions each day and can easily fall into trouble if they choose poorly.

While the research base is clear on which instructional strategies have an impact on student achievement, many teachers nonetheless choose very poorly for their students. It is incumbent upon a new teacher to learn a wide range of instructional practices and cull out the ones they may be familiar with that simply do not work.

Novice teachers should be leery of falling back to the kinds of instruction they experienced when they were students. That is not to say that historical teaching is suspect. Rather, it is the simple realization that familiarity is not the same as credibility. In the following scenario, the mentor teacher is reviewing the proposed lesson plans of her new student teacher, Ms. Whitley.

Mentor: Did you put some thoughts together for tomorrow's class?

Ms. Whitley: Yes, the curriculum guide suggested that we read a short story, so I picked one out of the anthology that seemed good.

Mentor: So what do you intend to do?

Ms. Whitley: Well, for starters, I was going to have them read a portion of it out loud and then have them finish it up on their own.

Mentor: So after they have finished the story, then what do you propose they do?

Ms. Whitley: I was going to put together a worksheet where they would have to fill in the blanks as they read the story to make sure that they were in fact reading it.

Mentor: And what purpose do you see that will serve?

Ms. Whitley: Well, I'm not certain that everybody is actually reading the assignments we have been giving them, so I figured this would ensure that they do. I don't see any way for them to answer the fill in the blank questions unless they are actually reading along.

Mentor: Do you see reading the story as the objective of today's lesson?

Ms. Whitley: Well, yeah, the curriculum guide suggested that they read it so I figured it was an appropriate activity.

Mentor: OK, that's a good start. But let me pull you back to the curriculum document itself. While you did capture the appropriate materials for today's lesson, you may have glossed over the underlying standard that we should be addressing when we use the short story. Do you see here where it cites the standard about identifying the main character's motivation and purpose in a work of fiction?

Ms. Whitley: Oh yeah, I guess I kind of forgot about the standard.

Mentor: Just remember that the standard needs to be the basis for the day's objective. If you are going to teach them how to determine the author's motivations using the short story, will you still have them do the fill in the blank reading guide?

Ms. Whitley: Not exactly. I guess my thinking on the reading guide was just to ensure that they had indeed read the story. But I am not sure that my idea for the reading guide was going to focus on the author's motivation in any sensible way.

Mentor: That's okay. We are now getting some place. If we are using the short story and we want them to work on the author's intent, can you think of any instructional strategy that may help? Think about some of the things that we have done so far this semester. Can you list some of the instructional protocols you have seen me use?

Ms. Whitley: Well, you have used Venn diagrams. You have used a fishbone activity. You have used that template to help them synthesize multiple texts. We did that Socratic seminar where they held a debate. I also remember when you had them do reciprocal teaching for the nonfiction, informational passages that they presented. I also remember you using a jigsaw strategy when they had to read longer passages.

Mentor: Good! Those are all very good strategies. But just because they are good does not mean that they would work best on every occasion. Can you think of which of them may work best for this?

Ms. Whitley: I'm not so sure.

Mentor: Let me ask you this, do you think a Venn diagram would work well for this task on determining the author's intent?

Ms. Whitley: No, as I remember it, the Venn diagram was used to compare and contrast two different things. Using that graphic organizer for this purpose does not seem to make much sense to me.

Mentor: I would agree. What else might you try?

Ms. Whitley: Wait a minute. What about the fishbone activity? You used it once to determine multiple causes and effects in a nonfiction passage. Couldn't

I modify it to diagram the different motivations the main character had that made him act the way he did? Wouldn't that work?

Mentor: That's a very clever idea, Ms. Whitley. I think you know the answer to the question yourself, though. What is the purpose of using the fishbone activity?

Ms. Whitley: It's the way to diagram multiple associated themes around a central idea with branching elaborations off it. I could diagram the multiple sources of motivation with text evidence supporting the claim branching off each idea. The more I think about it, I know I could make it work.

Mentor: I look forward to seeing you do it.

In this scenario Ms. Whitley received very good guidance from her mentor. To begin with, the mentor slowed down the overzealous young teacher who immediately gravitated toward the materials she intended to use in class. The mentor refocused her on the importance of beginning the lesson plan around a standard.

When the teacher had rooted her thinking back in the standard and then considered how to use the text around it, things started to fall into place. The mentor also noted that Ms. Whitley's first attempt at a task for the students to complete was merely one of compliance and unlikely to elicit deep thinking.

The mentor was not willing to allow Ms. Whitley to choose any instructional strategy. Instead, she suggested that the appropriateness of the instructional strategy has everything to do with the task at hand. A great instructional strategy may be the worst idea depending upon the circumstances.

Although Ms. Whitley had only witnessed a few instructional protocols at this point in her young career, she was able to pick a strong strategy and adapt it for the day's purpose. Student teachers can easily fall into the trap of recycling a handful of effective strategies and pressing them into service repeatedly. The student teacher in this scenario certainly chose an appropriate strategy but would be even better served if she had many more effective strategies in her own tool kit.

Expanding the available list of strategies should be a primary task for preservice teachers. With each strategy that they discover, they should also take thorough notes highlighting the occasion on which it is most useful.

After a teacher gains clarity on what they intend to teach and decides on how they intend to teach it, they then must have a thoughtful plan in place on how they will assess whether students have met the learning expectations. At times, educators inflate the topic of assessment into being much larger and more complicated than this.

In reality, assessment is nothing more than paying attention to and tracking the progress of students over time. Of course, this can be done in several ways. At times, educators seek to note the progress of students in very discreet and unobtrusive ways. On these occasions, informal methods of tracking student progress will suffice.

Teachers systematically work their way around the classroom, noting the concrete evidence of student learning that they observe and make an informal record of it. When this is done well, students often do not recognize that the teacher is assessing their work in these moments.

Of course, because students are very early in the learning process, and do not realize they are actually performing for their teacher, teachers must not use this data as anything more than an informal way of noting how students are progressing in that moment. Certainly, teachers need to make new instructional decisions based on the information they gather, but the information should not be used punitively by grading it on these occasions.

Other times, teachers want students to complete a task and make it clear that they are being assessed in the moment. This does not mean, however, that the teacher must automatically enter this as a graded task in the gradebook. On the contrary, teachers sometimes just want a more formal and comprehensive assessment of how each student is progressing.

Again, the purpose of this kind of assessment is simply to inform the teacher of the students' progress so they can make deliberate and intelligent decisions on how to proceed in their instruction.

In doing a cursory search, novice teachers will find that there are countless examples of quality formative assessments that they can use in their classrooms. To keep students engaged, it is appropriate to vary the formative assessment approach depending on the situation. This will also ensure that teachers capture the kind of information that they are truly seeking.

Even though these kinds of formative assessments are low stakes, they are still very important. In fact, it could be argued that they are the most important kind of assessment that is possible for a teacher to administer. Anytime a teacher is assessing and the results can inform the teacher on the next steps they need to take with the student, the value cannot be overestimated.

On occasion, teachers will also seek to assess their students in a summative manner. Teachers should remain very thoughtful in the type and frequency of summative assessments they give their students. This is especially true because teachers are compelled to give several district, state, and national tests as well.

Teachers should be thoughtful in any additional summative measures they give their students to prevent students from being overtested for less than thoughtful reasons. Certainly, there are occasions where teachers want to assess their students in a more formal way and need to record and preserve their grade.

Novice teacher should take great care that they do not assess students in a summative way as a method to mark time. *We just finished the chapter, I suppose I'd better give them a quiz.* Students should have had ample time and repeated opportunities to master the standards before they are assessed.

Only then is it fair and appropriate to memorialize a student's performance as a grade.

Preservice teachers should map out all assessments for the year on a timeline noting the summative measures that they are compelled to give. Further, the optional summative assessments that they choose to give should also be mapped against this timeline as well. Teachers should very clearly denote which assessments will be the basis for a student's grade and which assessments are simply ways to gather information about how a student is progressing. Confusing the two types of assessments is a colossal mistake that must be avoided at all costs.

Preservice teachers must keep a fine balance between curriculum implementation, instructional decisions, ongoing assessment, and thoughtful responses to student understanding. Juggling each of these aspects of education in a timely and thoughtful manner is a difficult task for all teachers. Student teachers must learn how to master each of these aspects of the profession, but also must do so within the context of all the other areas of responsibility. Each of the areas of the profession is connected with the rest. Making an adjustment to any aspect not only affects that dimension of the job but has implications for all other areas as well. No part of this work can be conducted in isolation.

When preservice teachers gain an understanding of each of these aspects of the job and work to implement them into an actual classroom full of students, the human dynamic and response is a critical dimension to the work. Teachers can make the mistake in assuming that this work will unfold nicely if they practice their work and commit to treating students well.

Although both ideas are essential, they are not sufficient. Teachers must also consider the structured way in which the classroom is organized. This, of course, is not a focus on the way in which the chairs in the room are organized. Rather, it is about the importance of presenting the acts of teaching in the way students actually learn.

The structure designed to complement how students learn has everything to do with whether students benefit from a solid curriculum and effective instructional approach. The strongest argument for instructional structure is to reflect upon the way in which young people (or anyone for that matter) learn how to do things in a natural environment.

Young people not only learn many complex skills outside of school but usually learn them from peers who have no formal training in teaching. Despite this fact, young people are very adept at helping their friends learn quickly and easily. Consider the conversation between two siblings as the older sister, Olivia, teaches, her younger sister, Sophie, how to ride a bike for the first time.

Olivia: Sophie, you should ride your bike with me.

Sophie: I can't. I don't know how yet.

Olivia: It's easy. I'll show you. Watch me! See how I'm doing it?

Sophie: But I can't do that, Olivia. I fall every time.

Olivia: Hop up on your bike and I will hold it steady for you. Grab the handlebars and put your feet on the pedals.

Sophie: Promise you won't let me fall?

Olivia: You won't fall. I'm holding on to you. Now, start pedaling and steer with your handlebars so you stay in the middle of the driveway.

Sophie: Like this?

Olivia: Yeah, you got it. Notice how you don't have to move your hands very much to keep it steady? If you move too much you will go all over the place.

Sophie: Okay, but please don't let me go.

Olivia: I have you. Don't forget to keep pedaling. You must steer and pedal at the same time. Do you feel how wobbly you get if you pedal too slow? You don't want to go too fast, but you can't go too slow either. Do you feel how you are tipping? Speed up just a little.

Sophie: Okay, I think I'm getting it. Can we practice a turn though?

Olivia: Sure, you're doing great. Okay, Sophie, I'm going to keep my hand on the back of your seat but I'm going to let go of your handlebars now.

Sophie: Please don't, Olivia. I'll fall.

Olivia: I can still hold you steady. See? You're steering all by yourself.

Sophie: Okay, but don't let go of my seat though.

Olivia: You've got this, Sophie! Let's practice left hand turns now, ok?

Sophie: I'm doing it, Olivia!

Olivia: Yes, you are! Guess what? I'm still walking beside you, but I haven't been holding on to you.

Sophie: Olivia! You promised you wouldn't let go.

Olivia: I said I wouldn't let you fall and you haven't. The whole point is to ride your bike by yourself and you are doing it!

Olivia is a master teacher. She may not know it, but she has mastered the critical structure supporting the way in which students learn. She begins her teaching lesson with an engaging hook to her learner to get her excited about the prospect of learning something new.

She continues her lesson by modeling what an exemplar performance of bike riding looks like. Sophie needed that mental picture to know what riding a bike properly looks like. However, bike riding is not ultimately learned as a spectator. Sophie needs to become an active learner, but Olivia needs to guide her learning in the early stages.

Olivia provides guided practice throughout the lesson. She watches her sister closely, offering feedback on what she's doing well and how to fix any mistakes she makes. Guided practice is at the heart of learning for students. It is in this stage that assessment feedback is critical. Olivia continuously assessed her sister's performance, but it was only for the purpose of helping her get better.

Ultimately, Olivia recognized that Sophie needed to be an independent learner. The goal of the bike riding experience is to be liberated beyond the driveway to ride without restriction. Likewise, students in any discipline have not completed the learning process if they are not able to function in the absence of the teacher.

Preservice teachers should reflect deeply upon how closely the masterful teaching practices of young Olivia are reminiscent of the school classroom. Olivia's method has stood the test of time and is the way in which anyone learns a new skill. Unfortunately, this system where responsibility of learning is gradually released to the learner through the thoughtful decisions of a teacher is not always found in public school classrooms.

If a teacher hands out a packet of worksheets and immediately tells students to use their book to answer the questions, the entire structure of the learning cycle is ignored. Although teachers must focus on content standards in their classroom using effective strategies to assist them, teachers must design the delivery of their instruction in a thoughtful way or learning will be less likely to happen. The structure is so simple that it occurs in driveways every night after school. *First, I'll do it. Next, we will do it. Then, you will do it.* Any departure from this system is likely to leave students behind in their learning.

Teaching is indeed both an art and a science. Teachers cannot teach what they do not know. What they know is much more than the content of the course. Rather, the craft includes thoughtful and responsive decision making on both what students must know and the best ways to ensure that they will learn. It requires such a nuanced and special set of skills that it ought to be considered a true craft. Without exception, teachers must learn this craft.

Chapter 6

The Power of a Reflective Notebook

As a preservice teacher begins to implement the most important aspects of teaching, it is important to reflect periodically on the progress and difficulties that become more apparent. Teachers can make the mistake of reflecting on the most difficult or frustrating experiences to serve as their measure of progress. This is a mistake. Negative experiences can emotionally hijack teachers and skew their ability to gauge their overall progress. Likewise, satisfying moments due to positive experiences can do the same.

Novice teachers need a way to track their performance and areas that need attention in a systematic and unbiased way. This will increase the likelihood that they are viewing their own subjective, lived experiences objectively. This is an important act of self-reflection that must be developed over time. This process will serve as a constant feedback loop for the teacher and it is not dependent solely on the mentor to provide advice and guidance.

Student teachers should begin this work by keeping a reflective journal of their progress as a student teacher. While it may be helpful for teachers to log their feelings around the successes and challenges they encounter, the journal must also serve as an objective tracking tool that is rooted in evidence and artifacts to inform the teacher of his next steps.

The first page of the reflective journal should be the self-assessment that the student teacher completed before the student teaching experience began. As each day passes and student teachers accrue more experience, their very understanding of the evaluation rubric is likely to evolve just as much as their belief about their growing proficiency.

On a frequent basis throughout the student teaching experience, teachers should reassess themselves on the rubric. This process should be a weekly ritual for the student teacher to complete. Reassessing at the end of each week ensures that bad habits do not form, and the areas of needed focus can be incorporated into the coming week's planning.

Preservice teachers should recognize that administrators are trained to collect evidence to support the evaluations they write for their teachers. This is done to remove subjectivity from the process and encourage teachers to accept the reality of their performance levels. This provides student teachers with a great opportunity. Because teachers do not need to rely on administrators to know if they are performing well, student teachers can assemble their own evidence of practice that supports their self-evaluation of proficiency.

If teachers desire that their administrators write their evaluations based on artifacts and evidence, then teachers should be willing to do the same in their own self-evaluations. Because the stakes are low for student teachers engaging in this sort of self-assessment, they should be willing to assess themselves based on evidence alone.

Teachers should begin this exercise by starting in the unsatisfactory category for each measured category of performance. This certainly takes some poise for teachers to begin with the notion that they are unsatisfactory in every area until they can provide evidence to prove otherwise. However, this is the only way to keep the process honest and prevent teachers' strong feelings about how good they want to be from skewing how well they are currently performing.

In a systematic fashion, student teachers should begin this process by reviewing the language of the evaluation rubric and considering what sort of evidence would show competency in that category. For example, if the category is *Communication with Families*, the student teacher should record the number of emails, phone calls, and personal visits that have been logged to date. The student teacher should then reflect on both the quality and the quantity of the communications. *Did I favor one method of communication over others? Have I engaged in two-way conversation or am I simply sending out mass emails? Do I have strong feelings about a student but have failed to engage in dialogue with parents about these concerns? How many contacts have I made per student? How many contacts am I averaging per week?*

These reflective questions should be guided by the language of the rubric describing the actions of a proficient teacher. Based upon the way the evidence weighs against the description of behavior, the student teacher should then mark the appropriate performance level.

Because student teachers are not yet experts in teaching, they may struggle to determine what kinds of physical evidence could be compiled to make these determinations. This is when teachers must reach out to mentors and administrators for assistance. By asking what sort of external behaviors would represent competency in each area, teachers can better understand their next steps.

Student teachers may rightly wonder whether they can expect to capture some time from their building administrator for insight and assistance. Principals are certainly busy, and some may indeed be reluctant to carve out time in their schedules for student teachers. However, there is an excellent way for student teachers to ensure that they can capture the attention of their administrator.

Teachers often make the mistake of requesting time in a principal's calendar to visit. This comes at the risk of a principal finding time to squeeze student teachers into their daily operations. Instead, student teachers should venture to reach out to their principals as they are completing their other work. For example, a principal may be unable to meet with a student teacher over her lunch hour because the principal must do lunch duty in the cafeteria. A wise student teacher would forgo her own lunch time and meet the principal in the cafeteria. Imagine the reaction of a principal if a student teacher were to say, "Good afternoon, Ms. Jenkins. Looks like you have your hands full here on lunch duty. I wondered if you would mind if I joined you today. Is there any way I could help you?"

As the student teacher begins to wipe down tables and pick up trash, the impression will not be missed by the principal who sees the student teacher voluntarily assist in one of the least favorite principal duties. Because the teacher isn't requiring the principal's exclusive attention, but is lightening her workload, an opportunity is created.

Whenever anyone willingly joins another in work that must be done (especially unpleasant work), a type of solidarity is formed. Joining principals in tasks such as playground duty, supervising the bus stop, and monitoring the halls is a powerful way to gain access to them. Because these tasks are largely supervisory, do not demand that the principal engage in other conversation, and are not mentally taxing, the principal is usually free and willing to fill the time with conversation. It is in these moments of sharing the workload that preservice teachers have the best opportunity to engage with the building leader.

The preservice teacher has made an incredible personal investment up to this point. Aside from at least four years of postsecondary academic preparation, student teachers are preparing themselves for approximately sixteen weeks of intensive preparation in front of students. After conducting the periodic self-assessments that constitute the beginnings of their reflective notebook, student teachers must also commit to backfilling other aspects of their preparation gaps outside of the classroom.

To this point, learning for the student teacher was on another's terms. Whether it be the course sequence they were required to take or the various assignments their collection of professors required, the learning was largely tailored for a mass audience. Everybody read the same articles and completed the same assignments. This may have served everybody well to a degree if the academic preparation was appropriate and rigorous. However, this approach does not take into account the particular strengths and weaknesses of each preservice teacher.

Every student teacher has gaps. Likely, these gaps are unpredictable and vary greatly depending upon the person. Because of this, student teachers are unable to address their preparation gaps with yet more generic assignments designed for a group. Instead, it is up to the individual student teachers to use their self-assessment and discern how they can best fill in their gaps.

Some of the gaps will likely be the need for more interpersonal interactions with young students. These gaps must be learned live in the classroom in front of students. However, some gaps are in requisite background information on the art and science of classroom instruction. These kinds of gaps may not be learned by repeated experiences in front of students.

For example, if a teacher recognizes his own shortcomings in asking rigorous questions of students, practicing low-level questions time and again will likely do little more than train the teacher to get better at asking weak questions. In this case, the answers are not to be found by spending more time with students. Instead, the teacher needs to do some more homework.

Fortunately, the investment a student teacher needs to make is not necessarily a financial one. The investment that is now required is indeed an intellectual one, but it may be done in different ways. Student teachers should consider how much they value their own education. This is a tricky question considering they are devoting their lives to the ideal that others should become lifelong learners. However, it is no secret that many teachers have largely abandoned their own learning.

How important is continual learning to me? Now that required article reviews and purchased textbooks are a thing of the student teacher's past, what role will learning now play for the student teacher? Every teacher will be quick to note that college preparatory programs are in no way capable of imparting everything a teacher ever needs to know as a professional. Student teachers must acknowledge that they do not even possess enough knowledge to span them through the first few years on the job. Teachers must pick up their own learning precisely where their college left off.

Often, educators will confess that they are not strong readers and do not enjoy reading. While this is undoubtedly true, it must be viewed as a temporary reality that must soon change. Not only must every educator embrace a love of reading to encourage students to do the same, but they must engage in professional reading outside of their students' view. If a student teacher is not a strong reader, he must practice.

Like everything in life, people get better at the things they practice. It is true for knitting a pair of mittens and it is true for becoming a stronger and quicker reader. The reason this is so important for the novice teacher is embedded in the lesson that every teacher of literacy recognizes. Reading is inhaling thoughts and writing is exhaling thoughts. The act of writing is the way in which people memorialize their thinking for others in another time and space. Because preservice teachers will likely have little personal access to the greatest thinkers in education, they have to acquire the learning through print.

Teachers pay thousands of dollars to listen to educational thinkers at live events and fail to realize that most of what they will ever learn can be read and reread repeatedly by picking up the speaker's latest book. Books are usually the basis of learning for a teacher's academic preparation program. Students learn so much from those books when they are in college. The learning can literally continue indefinitely by signing up for a free public library card.

The public library is a testament to the way society preserves and passes along the best thinking of our experts. If a library possesses thousands of titles, it also houses the equivalent of hundreds of master's and doctoral degrees. The learning a new teacher can acquire free of charge is simply amazing. Obviously, the books will not check themselves out, however. Preservice teachers must be active learners investing in furthering their own education at all times.

Of course, learning is not limited to print material only. This generation has been blessed with both audio books and a wealth of lectures and speeches on video. While a printed book has the benefit of being marked up and annotated in ways that can be referenced later, the method of delivery of further educational experiences is hardly the point.

What book is on the nightstand of the preservice teacher? What book has captured the attention to the degree that it is the last thing that is put down before closing her eyes at night? Preservice teachers should not feel compelled to choose between professional and leisure reading. Indeed, the learner should attack on multiple fronts. Perhaps the student teacher can commit to reading two books at a time. One book is for leisure, providing a release and distraction from the stress of their profession. The other book is one that challenges in the area where they need to grow the most as a professional.

Without question, student teachers could immediately compile a list of titles by simply asking other educators around them what book has most informed their practice. Imagine the accelerated learning that is possible for a teacher to read the five most consequential books recommended by the five strongest teachers in a building.

As student teachers compile their new list of resources that they should read to address gaps in their knowledge base, they should add these tasks into their list of evidence on their self-assessment. However, a teacher cannot simply note the books that she has read and feel confident that meaningful work has been accomplished. Instead, the reading becomes the foundation to implement new strategies within the classroom.

For example, if a teacher's self-assessment revealed weak skills in managing classroom behavior, the teacher should indeed seek out resources to build her repertoire of techniques for dealing with student behavior. However, that learning becomes meaningful only when it is applied in a classroom setting. Teachers should note the evidence of reading books about important skills but should then distill the learning from those books into actionable steps. Once those steps are recorded as evidence in the self-assessment, the teacher can then gather tangible evidence of improved performance in the classroom.

The process of self-assessing, gathering resources, distilling the lessons learned, implementing them in the classroom, and gathering evidence of their effectiveness must become a routine process that student teachers embrace as they systematically address their own weaknesses and improve their performance.

Student teachers should also recognize that books are not their only possible source for learning and improving as a professional. Student teachers also have the benefit of observing all those around them to see effective and ineffective practices. Certainly, preservice teachers begin their assignment by observing their mentor. However, what does it truly mean to observe another teacher?

If preservice teachers believe that observing a mentor is synonymous with watching them, they are likely to waste a lot of time. Within the context of the student teaching experience, novice teachers must become *critical observers* of their environment. A critical observer pays attention to everything going on around them. In earlier exercises, it was suggested that student teachers record the observations of their mentor, form hypotheses as to why the teacher made certain choices, and engage with the mentor in follow-up conversations to determine the real reasons for the observed behaviors.

The next step for preservice teachers is to add an additional element to their observations by beginning to anticipate and predict what should happen next in the classroom. For example, if the former practice was to watch the way in which a mentor intervened with a distracted student by using proximity as a technique, the student teacher must now make observations of what is happening in the environment *before* the teacher acts upon it.

With this advanced technique, the student teacher would have noticed the early warning signs of a student disengaging from the lesson. Before the teacher has a chance to respond, the student teacher should note the problem in his notebook and quickly make a list of possible ways to respond: proximity, verbally requesting the student to pay attention, asking the student a question to cue the need to re-engage. In the moments before the mentor intervenes, the student teacher must practice the technique of quickly considering possible responses.

Further, the student teacher needs to circle the intervention she would have made in that moment. It is one thing to consider the decision that another makes and decide how effective it worked in hindsight. It is quite another to commit to a response beforehand to see if it may match the way the teacher ultimately responds.

After the teacher responds to the noted behavior, the student teacher must then consider how effective the strategy seemed to be. If the mentor chose the same strategy that the student teacher suggested, the notes will simply reflect why it seemed to work. On occasion, the mentor may choose the same response as the student teacher, but the situation is not resolved or may worsen. In these moments, the student teacher needs to spend far more time reflecting on the reasons why a sensible response failed to bring about the desired outcome.

Often, the novice teacher will have very few strategies on the list they've created. This is incredibly informative in itself. If a student is disengaging from classroom instruction and teachers can only think of one or two ways to respond, the student teacher needs to make a notation that their inability to think of options suggests that they need to do more homework in the various responses that best practices prove effective.

Committing to a recommendation (on paper) of what the mentor ought to do before it happens reveals many things to a student teacher. It is easy to make a judgment of what has already occurred. Just as a novice chess player who barely understands the rules can follow the game of a chess master and concur with the best moves as they are unveiled, it is easy for a novice teacher to concur with the instructional decisions of the mentor. However, a whole new set of gaps are revealed in the novice chess players when they are presented with a board and asked to suggest the top four "candidate moves" they would consider if they were playing it. Having to commit to the best idea beforehand reveals a great deal.

To be a critical observer is to examine every option in a thorough and deliberate manner. Some may wrongly believe that to be critical is to be negative, but this is not the case or intent. By analyzing and critically examining the decisions made by the mentor teacher, the student teacher will learn and grow as a professional.

Primarily, by engaging in this activity repeatedly, moment by moment, throughout a lesson, student teachers will begin to appreciate the pace at which they must make important decisions within a classroom. These decisions will not be limited to responding to student misbehaviors. In each moment, a classroom teacher has a flood of questions running through his mind. *Who seems lost? Should I give another example? Do I need to change things up to prevent boredom? Is Mary paying attention? Does Justin have a frown on his face because he does not understand or is he upset about something?*

Coming to grips with the number of instantaneous decisions that need to be made is daunting for the novice teacher. However, student teachers must come to understand the reality of it from the very beginning. Because they cannot know the many internal conversations that are going on in the mentor's mind, they cannot make the mistake of failing to appreciate the number and frequency of decisions that must be made each moment. The best way to practice is to use this critical observation technique.

The second powerful lesson of the critical observation technique is that the listing of possible responses can reveal how few resources student teachers have in their own toolkit. By seeing how short the list of ideas is, student teachers can better understand where they need to do some more research and practice.

The most powerful outcome of the critical observation exercise comes in the deliberation of the response that the mentor tried. By observing both the mentor and the students with great scrutiny, the student teacher has the benefit of using the classroom as a laboratory of good practice. Watching firsthand which techniques work and when they work best in a live setting is far more beneficial that reading countless theoretical books on the topic. Moreover, by noting the mistakes that the mentor will inevitably make, observant student teachers can weed out ineffective practices before making the mistake themselves.

Student teachers should recognize that their role as a critical observer is not limited exclusively to classroom interactions with students. There are many other windows into the world of teaching and student teachers should take every opportunity to become critical observers in those areas as well.

When student teachers discuss planning with their mentors, they will invariably gain access (especially in the beginning) to the mentor's lesson plans. This is a rich source of learning for the novice teacher. Much like the classroom observations, student teachers should not simply read them and note the strengths of the mentor's planning. Instead, they should review the plans in stages.

To begin, student teachers should inquire which standards will be the focus of instruction in the coming week. The student teacher should then ask for a blank template that the mentor uses to produce her lesson plans. By just considering the standards that should be taught over the course of the week, student teachers should assemble their own planning document as well. Student teachers should keep in mind that quality lesson plans have many key components.

Regardless of whether the mentor uses a sensible planning template, student teachers should get in the habit of including several important features in their own planning design that should be woven into whichever template the mentor prefers. At the very least, quality lesson plans should include:

- Content standards being addressed
- Learning targets/objectives stating which portion of the standard will be taught that are written in student-friendly language

- Materials needed during the lesson
- Duration of the lesson
- Teacher-led instructional modeling including a strong opening "hook" to begin the lesson
- Scripted questions that the teacher will ask during the lesson
- Guided practice activities for students to attempt
- Types of formative assessments that the teacher will use to check for understanding
- Opportunities for independent practice of the day's skills
- A closure activity to end the lesson

The form and style that each of these component pieces takes is beside the point. Each of these items can be adapted to any lesson plan template. The underlying point, however, is that each of these pieces must be articulated in every lesson.

After completing a proposed lesson plan, the student teacher should then compare the plan against the mentor's prepared plans. Much like the critical observations of the mentor's teaching, the student teachers should evaluate the similarities and differences between their ideas and the mentor's.

Likely, the mentor will describe instructional protocols that are foreign to the novice teacher. Preservice teachers should take detailed notes and research the proven effectiveness and rationale behind each of these unknown strategies. This should be done before the student teachers see the instructional strategies unveiled in the classroom. When this is done, student teachers gain the benefit of knowing how the strategy was supposed to help students, and they can better determine if the strategy did indeed go as planned.

Perhaps the most powerful way that students learn is through descriptive and frequent feedback from their teacher. Fortunately, the student teacher has many opportunities to become a critical observer in this portion of the mentor's role as well. Student teachers will undoubtedly observe verbal feedback throughout their classroom observations and should record effective practices. However, the mentor will also give students significant written feedback through graded papers.

Preservice teachers should engage in a similar activity to the creation of lesson plans as they practice assessing student work. When teachers collect work from students, the student teacher should ask the mentor if she can make a copy of the student work to assess it herself.

Through a brief conversation with the mentor, the student teacher can ascertain what sort of feedback the teacher intended to give on a particular assignment. If the teacher intends to grade the assignment using a rubric or scoring guide, the student teacher should do the same. The point is that the student teacher should approach the feedback task in the same spirit that the teacher will.

After the mentor grades the work and supplies comments to the students, the preservice teacher should take a copy of the graded work and engage in the critical observation task of comparing feedback. *Was the feedback descriptive? Was it informative? Did I use vague, ineffective phrases such as "great job" or "try harder"? Did I note how the student could improve the work?* These are but a few of the critical questions that will assist a novice teacher's beginning attempts at providing student feedback.

The reflective notebook that a student teacher should put together is of critical importance. However, it should be noted that it is entirely optional. It won't be a required artifact for the student teacher to turn in as part of college coursework. Like many of the most important tasks in daily life, it is entirely optional. Telling a family member that you love them is optional, but it is very important. Eating a healthy diet is optional, but it is very important. Brushing your teeth is optional, but it is very important.

Student teachers must mature past the point where the only things worth considering are the required tasks. This reflective journal may be entirely optional but will likely be the most significant investment that can be made throughout the entire teaching experience. Self-assessment through personal reflection is an incredibly powerful teacher. This reflective notebook is a compilation of this focused thought and effort.

It should be reiterated that the notebook loses its power and effect if it is not done in a thorough and critical manner. The notations in this notebook could call into question many practices of the mentor. Because of this, it is important that the reflective notebook be for the student teacher's eyes only. While the purpose of the notebook is meant to be critical but not negative, any teacher whose practices are noted in the pages may not be so understanding of the words on the page.

This should not dissuade the student teacher from writing down completely honest and sharp insights when they arise. The purpose behind the criticism is not to hurt another. Because the reflective journal should not be shared with anyone, the student teacher should feel justified that the critical comments are serving a productive purpose.

When the notebook is complete, it will contain the paperwork chronicling the progression of a beginning teacher. Ensuring that the notebook begins with a critical self-assessment that is then systematically reviewed and readministered at regular intervals is mandatory. When this is done with fidelity and the teacher commits to addressing the gaps in evidence that are revealed with each passing self-assessment, there is no doubt that the preservice teachers will be able to see frequent and tangible progress in their skill level.

Repetition does not necessarily translate into better performance and technique. An old man may play the same tortured piano pieces over the course of a lifetime. He may make the same mistakes over and over again. He may play certain parts in a satisfactory way. However, he will not necessarily get better at the piece by simply playing it repeatedly. The old man will likely play the piece in his late seventies much the same way he played it in his early thirties.

This realization can be sobering, but there is a deeper insight hidden beneath the surface. Without systematic and focused practice, the old man will not only fail to improve his ability to play the piece, but he will certainly not improve as a pianist. A pianist is not someone who can play a song on the piano. How many songs must a person be able to play before it can rightly be claimed that he is, in fact, a pianist?

This lesson can be applied in all facets of life, but certainly extends to the role of a teacher. Someone handing out worksheets to students is not a teacher. Someone teaching the same lesson for twenty years in a classroom is not a teacher with twenty years of experience. The difference that matters resides in the focus and commitment that teachers brings to their craft.

Because it may be very difficult for student teachers to judge the effectiveness of the teachers around them, they should exercise the sort of methodical caution that the reflective journal values. Before a student teacher adopts a practice simply because another teacher suggests it, she can certainly run the idea through the critical observation filter.

What practice is being suggested? What purpose would it serve? Is it likely to bring about the desired effect? Might there be a superior strategy to the one suggested? How might I do more research on the effectiveness of the suggestion? If it is an idea worth pursuing, how will I know if it was successful? These are the kinds of self-reflective questions that can give student teachers their bearings early on in their classroom experience when they may not be sure of what is worth trying.

Getting better at any skill takes time to master. Teaching is no different. Many expert teachers have invested their entire adult lives to the practice of teaching and still uncover areas of needed focus and improvement. While becoming a master teacher takes a great deal of time and attention, significant improvements in teaching ability are quite possible in a relatively short amount of time. However, it never happens by accident.

The reflective notebook ensures a commitment to focused effort and systematic reflection of a teacher's skills as she progresses over time. The process values the mentoring that the cooperating teacher can provide. The student teacher must never forget the great gift that the mentor provides by opening up the classroom. Mentor teachers are not perfect. The student teacher will likely see them make many mistakes over the course of their time together. It is important for the preservice teacher to remember the importance of being easy on people and critical of ideas. The reflective notebook is an exercise in collecting the best and sorting out the worst ideas that make an appearance in the classroom.

Above all, student teachers are compelled to be forgiving of imperfect mentor teachers. Mentor teachers, like most teachers in the profession, are doing the best they know how in the given stress of the moment. While student teachers should be forgiving of imperfect people, they should be relentlessly unforgiving of imperfect practices. The reflective notebook is the most powerful weapon a new teacher has in identifying what practices should be embraced and which practices must be banished.

Chapter 7

Building a Better Portfolio

When preservice teachers move past the belief that the student teaching experience is limited to student contact they have during the weeks they are assigned to the classroom and embrace the reality of the monumental work that must be invested, it is easy to become overwhelmed. The work that should be done to ensure thorough preparation for a proper transition into the teaching profession will require countless hours outside of the classroom.

The months spent student teaching are also the months leading up to the application and interview process for prospective teachers. The investment to become a teacher should amp up in the weeks and months before the hiring season. Unfortunately, many prospective teachers begin to wind down their preparation in advance of securing interviews.

Because time is short, student teachers should look for every possible occasion to squeeze extra hours and opportunities into their teaching experience. The time in which students are in session is the most precious commodity in their professional lives at this point. The opportunity to observe, instruct, and tutor students is fleeting for the student teacher. There is no time to waste.

Unfortunately, student teachers often waste this precious instructional time by failing to seize additional opportunities within the school day. The biggest mistake that student teachers can make with their time is to mirror the schedules that their mentor teachers keep. Mentor teachers have full-time jobs and have certainly earned the right to their preparatory periods and duty-free lunches. Student teachers cannot afford to sit idle during these times.

Preservice teachers must be willing to make short-term sacrifices for long-term gains during their student teaching experience. For example, teachers typically get preparatory periods each day to tend to such things as getting their lessons and materials put together for the following day, grading papers, and perhaps even resting a bit to catch their breath to finish the remainder of the day.

Student teachers should always ask their mentor if they can help put together lessons or make copies during this prep time. At times, they may indeed be a helpful extra set of hands for their mentor. On other occasions, mentor teachers may not desire that every possible minute be spent engaged with their student teacher. From the very beginning of the student teaching experience, preservice teachers should ask their mentors if it is acceptable to go visit other classrooms when their presence is not required.

Using preparatory time in this way seizes an important block of time to observe other teachers. However, student teachers should also look for other periods of time when their presence in the classroom is not demanded. For example, teachers usually get a short block of time for lunch each day. While this period of time is usually not very long, it is time that student teachers would not be supervising their own students.

Student teachers must ask themselves if they are willing to limit their lunch break to the few minutes it would take to eat a sandwich and then re-deploy themselves in other classrooms. Even if limited to an additional twenty-minute segment, this extra time would equate to over twenty-six hours of observation time over the course of a sixteen-week student teaching assignment. Gaining twenty-six hours of additional experiences is the kind of edge that can make the difference in securing a position and beginning a teaching career with additional skills.

Novice teachers have an incredible opportunity to expand their observational base if they seize these spare periods of time. Because student teachers are assigned to one mentor who has a predetermined schedule, the experiences that student teachers get will normally be limited to that particular grade or course. If student teachers are able to get released during prep periods or lunch time when their tasks are completed, the entire school can be opened up to them.

In the following scenario, Mr. Richards engages with his mentor in a candid conversation about his desire to expand his experiences:

Mr. Richards: I finished laying out the materials for tomorrow's lab. Is there anything else I could be doing for you right now?

Mentor: No, I think that's about it. I'm just going to finish reading this journal article and rest for a bit before 4th hour starts.

Mr. Richards: Do you think it would be okay if I were to run next door and observe Ms. Perkins? She is teaching Physics right now and I have been wondering how the students in that class differ from our freshmen Biology students. I asked her last week if she'd be okay if I stopped by.

Mentor: Yeah, no problem. I have no doubt you'll see a bit of a difference between the two courses!

Mr. Richards: I was wondering if there were any other sections I might visit when we have some down time?

Mentor: Yeah, I have a couple of ideas right off the bat. Mr. Conner teaches a collaborative section of Physical Science right now. It is comprised of a mix of special education students. That is the same course as ours but you might be interested in seeing that section.

Mr. Richards: Anything else come to mind?

Mentor: Truthfully, you need to go watch Mrs. Palmer teach.

Mr. Richards: I don't know her, I guess.

Mentor: She's not a science teacher. She teaches Human Geography. You need to see more than just science. Mrs. Palmer is the best teacher I've ever seen. You should watch her for a few minutes and see how you might apply her approach in your own style.

Mr. Richards: Do you think she'd mind?

Mentor: I'd ask her first. The best teachers likely won't mind, but it is always a good idea to give them a heads up.

Mr. Richards: Great idea. Will you also make it clear to me when you'd like me to stay and help you during your prep and when you're okay if I venture out to other classes?

Mentor: Absolutely. Keep in mind that there are some preparatory skills that you need to practice too. But by and large, you'll have plenty of time to venture out on observations if you want to do that.

Mr. Richards begins this conversation in a very healthy way. Before making a request of his mentor, he first establishes that he has met the expectation of the moment. This is important in maintaining a healthy relationship with a mentor that is based on open and clear communication. Student teachers should never give the mentor the impression that they are skirting their primary responsibilities.

The student teacher also handles the conversation wisely by noting that he would like to observe other students to gain additional experiences. Mentor teachers are human, and their pride can be easily wounded just like anyone. By making it clear that Mr. Richards is seeking to observe different students, it eases the conversation into a place where the mentor begins to consider the other experiences that may be healthy for the student teacher to observe.

This approach avoids the unfortunate circumstance that can arise where the mentor feels threatened that the student teacher is seeking to form a primary teaching relationship with someone else. The student teacher needs to reassure the mentor that he desires extra experiences rather than a different mentor. By actively debriefing with the mentor about the experiences he observes, Mr. Richards will pull his mentor into the conversation rather than alienating the mentor.

The conversation Mr. Richards has initiated also serves the purpose of getting the mentor to think of the supervisory role in a different way. It is easy for the mentor to think of the role as one where the student teacher shadows the mentor with a gradual release of responsibility to the point where the mentor observes the student teachers as the primary instructor of the class. While this is certainly a healthy way to view the student teaching experience, it fails to account for the breadth in opportunity within a school setting.

The student teacher should not view the request of Mr. Richards as simply a professional way to ask permission to observe other teachers. It is also an opportunity to tap into the wisdom of the mentor in sharing opinions of other educators and experiences that could be valuable. The student teacher should be a collector of experiences. The mentor will certainly supply many of those experiences but can also point the student teacher in other directions to collect additional experiences.

What then should student teachers do with all of these experiences and opportunities they are able to gain during their student teaching assignment? Student teachers are at a point where they can begin compiling all of the resources they have been collecting. They have captured three-column notes that served as a conversation starter with their mentor on why certain decisions were made. They have kept a reflective journal to anticipate best practices and critique observations they have made. They have conducted numerous self-assessments tracking their progress as they make gains within the classroom. They have also begun collecting outside experiences and opportunities that can expand their skills.

All these pieces can now be brought together to begin assembling a professional portfolio. Many educators view a professional portfolio as a collection of formal documents to give an employer. Many colleges would suggest a binder filled with letters of recommendation, a statement describing a student's philosophy of education, and a sample lesson plan as being the sort of portfolio that would impress an employer. This sort of portfolio never paints a true picture of a student teacher's true skills and never separates one candidate from another.

It is important for a student teacher to place himself in the position of a hiring team. Might anyone effectively argue that a student is going to write a philosophy of education that is somehow superior and more memorable than every other candidate? The answer is no. Nearly every philosophy of education statement is the same.

Student teachers must assemble a portfolio that represents what they are truly able to do. Once again, referring to the evaluation instrument of their school district is the best place to begin. By using the instrument that delineates each of the important aspects of teaching ensures that a student teacher systematically keeps track of each area.

Preservice teachers should put together a binder that has tabs marking each area of the evaluation instrument. Obviously, in the beginning, the sections will be empty. This is the challenge for the student teacher: fill each section with a meaningful artifact. Student teachers should recognize that this portfolio begins as a useful tool for them and the portfolio that they will bring to an interview may be slightly different.

Each artifact that a student teacher puts into the designated section of the portfolio must be personalized. For example, traditional portfolios often include lesson plans. In the age of technology where countless resources are available instantaneously, what does including a lesson plan really prove? If a student teacher included a quality lesson plan, a hiring committee may know that the teacher recognizes quality work. However, there is nothing to suggest that the teacher actually wrote the lesson plan.

That is not to suggest that a lesson plan is not worth including. Indeed, one of the sections of the professional portfolio is likely to be on a teacher's ability to plan for instruction. Although including a generic lesson plan is a bad idea, student teachers can personalize a lesson plan in powerful ways.

Because a lesson plan can be so easily borrowed from another educator, student teachers must make it their own. The best way to do this is to treat the lesson plan as a living document. The lesson plan is the way a teacher prepares for instruction. Educators quickly realize that they typically depart from their planned lesson nearly as soon as they begin. This is because the plan plays out in the lives of students and teachers must respond to how students progress through the proposed lesson.

Imagine if a teacher assembled a quality lesson plan and then annotated it based upon the adaptations he had to make as the lesson progressed. As students struggled to grasp the lesson, the teacher responded by re-grouping and re-teaching the lesson in significant ways. As the teacher formatively assesses students throughout the lesson, it usually becomes clear that some of the strategies and activities did not go well. The student teacher should annotate those items noting the deficiencies. Likewise, many activities work very well and should be retained for the next time the lesson is taught. The teacher should make notes on these aspects of the lesson as well.

In the end, a student teacher has a pristinely typed lesson plan that has then been marked up nearly beyond recognition. If an administrator were to look at this document, it would paint a powerful picture. Rather than wondering if the teacher plagiarized someone else's lesson plan, the principal would see a thoroughly constructed plan that has been modified in light of actual student performance. This tells an entirely different story. This tells a highly personalized story of the student teacher's skills.

The example of a lesson plan provides tangible document that can be added to a professional portfolio. There are other examples that fit into this category as well. For example, a teacher could produce several informal formative assessments that were completed by students based upon a predetermined learning target. This would provide an employer with definite insight into how the teacher is able to break a standard into a student-friendly learning target that is ultimately used to assess students in a low-stakes format.

Student teachers need to develop a keen eye for opportunities that arise in class that provide appropriate artifacts for the professional portfolio. However, one piece of evidence is not enough for each category of the evaluation instrument. Instead, teachers should add to the portfolio additional examples they are able to compile throughout the student teaching experience. Certainly, inferior pieces of work can be removed when superior artifacts are developed. Having multiple examples for each section is most desirable though.

Student teachers should take care to assess the form in which an artifact ought to be collected. For example, teachers will most certainly need to collect artifacts that demonstrate the communication and connections they have made with families. There are a few possible ways that the teacher could collect examples for this category. The student teacher could easily track the number of phone calls, emails, and face-to-face meeting held with parents.

In an interview setting, a hiring committee could easily ask about the candidate's belief around the importance of communication with parents. Because of the tracking artifacts that the student teacher compiled, she could easily add a concrete example of her commitment to communication. Note the difference between the following two responses when questioned about communicating with families:

Communicating with families is very important in establishing a partnership in the education of a child.

Communicating with families is very important. During my student teaching experience, I made 157 phone calls to parents. I usually average two calls per day. I called each parent more than five times each. I contacted every parent during the first week of my assignment to introduce myself.

I varied subsequent calls between positive calls and the unfortunate calls required to help parents understand how their child was struggling. I also emailed parents on a regular basis providing updates on what we were doing in class each week. I also held eight face-to-face meeting during my assignment.

As you know, sometimes conversations need to happen in person. I believe I developed strong relationships with my parents during this time. I believe it shows how I truly partnered with parents in their child's education.

Certainly, the first response is accurate and positive. However, it lacks any depth and is likely to be quickly forgotten by a hiring committee. The second response elaborates on the types of communication and the reason for meeting with parents. Principals will likely be encouraged by the second teacher's genuine efforts to partner with parents.

Student teachers may wonder if simply tallying up the number of forms of communication paints the complete picture. Might there be additional artifacts that the teacher could collect to share with others? Obviously, relaying the substance of a telephone conversation would be awkward and contrived in an interview setting. However, capturing a piece of written communication with a parent could be useful instead.

Suppose a student teacher redacted the personal information out of the following email to a parent:

> I wanted to take moment to give you some updates on Maria's progress in class. We were working on argumentative essays this week and your daughter chose to focus her paper on bullying in schools. I cannot begin to tell you how fine of a job she did on her paper. She provided a thoughtful synopsis of the issue and the challenges that schools face. When she presented it to the class, every student was completely captivated by her arguments. In fact, I heard one student suggest that she should give a copy of it to the principal, so she could consider some of the suggested solutions.
>
> This was truly the best work I've seen her produce all year. As I reflected on her work, I couldn't help but worry about the consistency she has demonstrated in her school work. Sometimes, she just doesn't seem as connected and engaged as she was on this assignment. Of course, my goal for her would be to achieve at levels every day like she did on our latest assignment.
>
> I wondered if you had noticed the same patterns of ups and downs with Maria at home or whether you have a theory on why this might be happening. As you know, I think the world of her and would appreciate any insight you may have on how we can partner together to make my class a great experience for her every day.

This short email would probably take less than five minutes to write but speaks volumes about the student teacher. Primarily, it establishes a strong and positive connection between the teacher and the parents. Parents obviously love to hear the way in which their child excels in the classroom.

Of course, the teacher also takes the opportunity to share a concern she has with Maria's performance in school. It should be noted that the concern does not eclipse the positive tone and feedback of the email. Parents will likely receive the communication in the spirit in which it was sent: Maria is doing well. She is capable of greatness. The teacher would like to see more consistency in her performance. She'd like to partner with the parents to help Maria be even more successful.

A principal reading this email would not need to meet Maria or her parents to appreciate the type of relationships that this teacher fosters and values. This artifact gives a qualitative feel of the teacher's skills in addition to the quantitative summary the teacher previously gave regarding the number of contacts she had made.

Preservice teachers should thoughtfully consider the various forms of artifacts that they can gather for each aspect of the teaching experience. However, some areas of practice may be more difficult to capture in a tangible way. The student teacher should not conclude that these areas of instructional practice do not require artifacts. Rather, the form that the artifact takes simply needs to be a bit different.

For example, one important aspect of teaching is the ability of teachers to manage student behavior within the classroom. In contrast to the examples above, it would not be appropriate to tally up all the student misbehaviors that the teacher observed and handled. Likewise, capturing a paperwork artifact of an office referral for misbehavior would not make sense either. How then could a student teacher paint the picture of the way discipline is handled in the classroom?

Likely, hiring committees will focus one of their interview questions on this particular topic. Most student teachers will respond to a question about managing student behavior in the following way:

> In order to maintain an environment conducive to learning, I believe that students must demonstrate mutual respect to me and their peers. I believe in being proactive and will always give the student additional chances to meet my behavioral expectations.

If a student teacher does not answer in this way, it will likely be a close variant. There is always lots of talk of respect and dignity while maintaining a learning environment. Is this approach so wrong?

There is nothing wrong with a statement like this, but it hardly separates one candidate from the next and every answer will be quite similar. If a candidate can answer a question in a way that could also be true for the next candidate in line, that teacher has more work to do in crafting an answer.

The artifact that a teacher needs to collect for these areas of performance will never be written on paper. The required artifact is a compelling story. Instead of offering a sterile description of a well-managed classroom, the student teacher needs to paint a picture of what it looks like for her to deal with a student misbehavior.

Imagine that the student teacher answered the question on managing student behavior in a way that draws upon a personal story collected from the student teaching experience:

> I'm glad you asked me a question about classroom management. It is such an important topic especially for new teachers. I had a student named James who challenged me particularly during my teaching experience.
>
> One day while I was leading a classroom discussion, James wadded up a piece of paper and threw it at another student and began cursing at her. I recognized that James was having a moment like others I had witnessed with him before. I quickly got between James and the other student and leaned down and asked James to meet me in the doorway.
>
> He complied but shoved his chair across the room as he did. I directed one of the students to continue reading the passage that was the basis for our discussion. I positioned myself in the doorway so I could continue to monitor the class and spoke in a firm but quiet voice, so the others could not hear what I was saying.
>
> I reminded him that his outburst was in violation of his behavior plan and asked if he remembered how we agreed to respond if he interrupted the learning of the class. He admitted that he'd be escorted to the office to speak with the principal by my teaching assistant. He then quietly walked out of the room and I followed up with the principal after class.

This student teacher painted a compelling picture of classroom management in a few brief statements without resorting to dramatic effect. Those on the hiring committee would quickly learn that this teacher understood the importance of proximity in redirecting a student misbehavior. Additionally, the teacher sought to remove the student from the aggravating circumstance but did so without escalating the student and without humiliation to the student who misbehaved.

The teacher also recognized the importance of keeping the other students in a learning environment while she dealt with the situation. She also communicated the importance of continuing to supervise the rest of the class while visiting with James. Her reference to an established behavioral plan indicated her intimate knowledge in how to respond to James' outbursts in a calm and predictable manner.

This response from the teacher is an artifact of her teaching experience. The artifact is a well-crafted story illuminating a typical interaction she had with students. The first statement about classroom management will quickly be forgotten. The interview committee will not forget about James. They know someone like James. As she told her story, they began to fill in the details on her behalf. James had a face and that face will not be quickly forgotten.

Student teachers must collect a combination of both tangible artifacts when possible and detailed examples of their performance when it is not. As student teachers complete their professional portfolio, they would be wise to quickly draft a narrative of which stories they would tell to highlight their performance in a particular area. While they should not read the exact narrative to a hiring team, they do need to add the sort of details to their story that would paint a picture full of depth and detail.

Preservice teachers must create one last section of their professional portfolios apart from all the components of their evaluation system. This section should be entitled: Student Work. In this section, student teachers should collect and organize samples of their students' work over the course of their student teaching assignment.

This is the most critical and consequential section of the portfolio. It is imperative that student teachers begin collecting student work from the first days of their teaching experience. Obviously, student teachers need to ask permission of their mentors before making copies of this work. Also, student teachers should redact any identifying information about the student. When identifying information is removed, mentor teachers usually feel far more comfortable in allowing student teachers to create a scrapbook of student work.

The collection of work must take a definite form. The purpose of this section of the portfolio is not to capture exemplary student work. Rather, the purpose is to capture student growth in performance over time.

While student teachers should certainly redact student names from the work, they must organize the collected work by student in some identifiable form. Throughout the course of the student teaching assignment, preservice teachers should look at comparable samples of student work and detail the growth that is apparent from piece to piece. With sticky notes affixed to different aspects of an assignment, student teachers should note the specific areas of student improvement. Is there improvement in the student's vocabulary? Is the student writing more complex sentences as the semester goes along? Is the student now supplying evidence from the text when supporting an answer?

The student teacher must show specific before and after examples in student progress. Further, the work should also include specific feedback in the margins that the teacher gave to the student to improve the work. When done properly, each student has samples of inferior work product with descriptive notations in the margins giving them suggestions for improvement followed by subsequent examples of that student's work that is of higher quality.

This section of the portfolio will undoubtedly be the most powerful thing a student teacher can produce during the student teaching experience. More important than a resume or exemplary letters of recommendation, an organized sample of student work is the most significant artifact in any teacher's portfolio.

The reason why this is true is readily apparent. The primary purpose of the classroom teacher is to facilitate high levels of student learning. Although it is indeed important to establish good rapport with the students and to partner with their parents, all other aspects of teaching lead to the ultimate purpose of student achievement. All other aspects are necessary, but nothing is sufficient in the absence of authentic learning.

The student work portfolio proves in a very tangible and visceral way that students will learn when placed under this teacher's care. The before and after nature of the samples shows the best attempt possible before instruction and the results after instruction. Educators fully recognize that many students are not learning each day. Learning never happens by accident.

When educators can witness the transformation of student performance from novice to master of an important educational standard, no further argument needs to be made. The student teacher can confidently state, "Learning is essential. The only thing that happened to this student between these two pieces of work is that I entered his life. If you entrust students to my care, I can promise you that they will learn. Let me show you examples of what this looks like with real students."

Student teachers must begin work on their professional portfolio, modifying it with each passing day. It is the very scrapbook proving their worth as novice teachers. It is the place where they reflect on their own strengths and weaknesses. It sorts out best and worst instructional practices in a systematic way. It serves as the evidence of which things the teacher does well and where she needs more practice. Above all, it captures and memorializes the learning that has occurred with young people during the student teaching assignment.

This professional portfolio has its beginnings as a tool for the student teacher to learn and grow. After it has been completed, the student teacher can then turn attention to pulling out the best of it as the basis for artifacts to share with a hiring committee. If the student teacher has been thorough and diligent in the process, preparing for upcoming interviews will present far less stress and require less preparation than one might expect.

Chapter 8

The Application Process

When student teachers put concerted efforts into assessing, tracking, and developing the necessary skills to account for all important aspects of teaching, they can be sure that they are doing everything they can do prepare themselves to enter the profession. However, the investment they have made in themselves ultimately needs to be communicated to the professionals who will hire them for vacant positions.

Student teachers are at a distinct disadvantage in this regard as they have very limited access to the thinking that is valued by those who hire teachers. Teachers can be reassured that they can anticipate many steps that they should take in keeping with proper preparation. Although many of the steps a hiring team may consider in weighing a candidate's strengths are not surprising, a novice teacher may not necessarily think of them without specific prompting.

One fundamental truth of any hiring process is that before a team decides who they want to fill a given position, they first determine who they do not want to hire. Depending upon the position and the location in the country, employers may get several dozen applications for each vacancy.

Principals will rarely interview more than five candidates for a particular position. Because the interview process is time intensive, only a select few will survive the culling process and receive an interview call. How then can a prospective teacher survive the application process?

It may seem a bit unfair that a candidate could be judged before even meeting with a hiring team. The reality of the situation is that many highly desirable teaching candidates never make it past the application phase. Principals simply do not have the time to give candidates the benefit of the doubt if they put together a weak application.

Fortunately, there are many things a teacher can do to survive this process and increase the chances of securing an interview. Because screening committees approach the initial task by screening out the candidates they do not want before deciding which ones they do wish to interview, candidates need to avoid the kinds of mistakes that will immediately result in rejection.

Prospective teachers must fully understand the way in which a school system accepts and handles applications. Most school districts utilize an electronic application having interested teachers apply online. As soon as the submit button is clicked, teacher applicants will no longer have control of what they typed in the blanks. Because of this, it is important to ensure correct spelling, use proper grammatical conventions, and format the text in the way that the application requires. For any lengthy narratives, candidates should first type their answers in a word processing document to take advantage of built-in spelling and grammar checking aids.

Answering every required question on the application is also essential during the application process. If the application inquires if the school can contact a former employer, a blank or negative response becomes a huge red flag for an employer. It is possible a teacher had a bad experience with an employer and would prefer they not be contacted. In this case, an additional piece of narrative explaining the situation is needed while still permitting the school to contact them. If a prospective employer is told that they cannot speak to a reference, it will probably be a sufficient reason to pass on the applicant.

If the application allows letters of recommendation to be submitted, the applicant should attach them. Missing information paints a picture that will likely not be worth keeping a candidate in the pool. Student teachers should give their references plenty of advance time to assemble a letter of recommendation. A letter that is written in haste will not likely be as flattering as one given sufficient time.

Prospective employers are realistic in their understanding of the kinds of letters a new teacher will be able to gather. Because student teachers' experiences are limited, they may not be able to get letters from district-level administrators. However, the student teacher should actively solicit a letter from both the supervising mentor teacher and the building principal.

By inviting the school principal for several observations throughout the student teaching experience, the student teacher will ensure the principal has a strong basis to write a consequential letter. These visits should be short and focused on a compelling lesson or activity. By keeping a discrete focus for observations, student teachers will provide the principal with specific examples that can be worked into the letter without demanding too much of the principal's time.

For example, a student teacher in social studies may ask the principal to come observe a brief debate students will be conducting based upon a review of historical primary source documents. When the principal uses this as an example in the letter of recommendation, it will provide specific details rather than producing a generalized letter with little appeal.

Principals are incredibly busy professionals and writing a letter of recommendation adds to their workload. The best way to minimize the inconvenience for them is to give them plenty of advance notice before the letter is needed and to provide a detailed bulleted list of the essential experiences the student teacher hopes that the principal's letter will capture. By providing some of the details in advance, the principal may feel like much of the substance of the letter is available and does not need to be created from whole cloth.

By supplying a resume and list of applicable experiences to those who may write a letter of recommendation, student teachers do not leave their superiors with the impression that they are casting a wide net in securing letters. It is much easier to ask for a letter than to write one. Showing colleagues that a measure of work has gone into assisting them write the letter is a worthwhile sign of partnering in the work.

Before submitting any paperwork to a prospective employer, a prospective teacher should make a wager with someone in her life who is close enough to be brutally honest. The wager is that the student teacher will buy the friend or colleague lunch if they can find an error in her paperwork. A discerning eye that is tuned in to finding mistakes is invaluable at this stage of the application. A principal may not spend more than a few minutes reviewing the paperwork. Typically, the first error that the principal finds will be enough to winnow the pile of applications down to a workable number. Student teachers should never give someone the reason to reject their paperwork. Survival in the process is required before one gets the opportunity to convince a team that she is the best candidate for the position.

A resume will undoubtedly be a part of the application process as well. This document is a quick way for a hiring team to learn about a candidate. Because they are likely looking at more than twenty applications, prospective teachers should ensure that the resume works to their benefit and not their detriment.

A resume is a professional document being reviewed by an employer. Teachers should refrain from childish fonts or graphics adorning the document. Even if a teacher is applying for a job working with young children, principals think of their teachers as professionals first. There will be a time to decorate bulletin boards in an inviting way for students. During the application process, teachers should stress that they are consummate professionals fully prepared to handle the rigors of the teaching profession.

A resume should be arranged in a manner that meets the expectation of those reviewing it. It should have clearly defined categories highlighting an applicant's prior education, work experiences, honors, and relevant skills.

The resume font should be highly readable and of sufficient size for older eyes to read easily.

An applicant can get caught up in the details written on the page of an application and may forget that the resume will be viewed at a distance before being read close up. Much like a work of art, a good resume balances its use of space ensuring that there are no giant blocks of text on the left margin with large chunks of white space on the other half of the page.

The resume should also be reviewed to ensure that the same number of spaces exist throughout the document for each section. If the resume has a larger text size for headings, that size should be standardized throughout the document. An applicant should be consistent in descriptions of each entry on the document. If bulleted points are complete sentences, they should be punctuated accordingly. If they have verbs, they should have strong active verbs. Consistency is key for each entry in the document.

Novice teachers can make the mistake of underestimating some of the experience they do have even though they have never been a full-time educator. Student teachers should be very thorough in the explanation of the experiences and duties they performed during their teaching experience. If a candidate was able to be an active member of Individualized Education Program (IEP) meetings for special education students, he should highlight that experience.

Every student teaching experience is unique and some experiences a student teacher receives are not typical. Highlighting every experience takes advantage of the opportunity to begin separating a student teacher from others seeking the position. Committee work, professional development, and extra duty assignments are all key highlights to be included on the resume.

Ideally, student teachers will create an initial draft of their resume very early in their student teaching experience. Much like the self-assessment, a lean resume can show teachers areas where they may need to add additional opportunities for themselves.

For example, a student teacher may not have very many entries in her work history at an early point in her career. However, work experience is not limited to paying jobs only. If a teacher becomes a volunteer coach for Special Olympics, it should have an entry on the resume. Teachers willing to donate spare time to helping others will have no problems filling out a resume in a respectable way even if they have never held a full-time job in education.

Teachers cannot underestimate the powerful message that volunteering sends. When a principal notes volunteer experience, it makes a few important impressions. Primarily, a principal appreciates that the experience was optional. When a person donates time to a good cause without financial compensation, it begins to paint a picture of the sort of applicant who is seeking employment.

Suppose a principal has a nephew who is profoundly handicapped? How might seeing a Special Olympics coaching experience on an application endear the candidate to the principal immediately? All people look for connections and common causes to unite them. Volunteer work can be a meaningful way to connect with others who have only met an applicant on paper.

When candidates discover portions of the resume that could be bolstered, they should take necessary steps to fill in the blanks. Even employment opportunities from one's youth can be helpful on a resume. A prospective teacher may get tunnel vision and suppose that a principal is only interested in experience within the classroom. This could not be farther from the truth.

If a candidate has military experience, she should highlight that professional responsibility. When a principal sees that on a resume, she immediately recognizes that the applicant likely excels in team leadership, discipline, and the importance of accomplishing goals. These qualities are obviously valued in the classroom.

If an applicant's work experience is in the service industry, it is important to note the valuable skills that are acquired in these jobs as well. If an applicant worked as a waitress through college, it paints the picture of someone who can handle a busy work environment working with difficult and needy people. These too are skills that are valued in the classroom.

Teachers must make the connections come to the surface, however. Simply noting experience in the workforce is not enough. Applicants should examine the skills that are necessary in that job and highlight those that have a usefulness in the classroom.

The resume is an opportunity to paint the picture that the applicant is worth getting to know further. Because the applicant is simply trying to survive the process at this time, no detail is too small. Many applications have been discarded simply because the contact email address for the applicant seemed juvenile or provocative.

In addition to a resume, every application will also include a cover letter. Cover letters tell a bit more of the applicant's story than the resume. While the two documents complement each other, there are important distinctions.

A cover letter is personalized to the intended recipient. If a teacher is applying to twenty different schools, she must commit to writing twenty distinct cover letters. There are ways to do this in an efficient way so that the entire letter does not need to be rewritten each time, but each letter must be written with each school in mind. A cover letter is a prime opportunity to make a connection with a potential employer. However, if an applicant gets an important detail incorrect, it can also be an instantaneous way to end up in the rejection pile.

For example, if a cover letter is addressed to the wrong person, that can be quite insulting. Addressing a letter to the former principal of a school will likely send a message that the applicant makes mistakes in small matters. Can the one unable to attend to small matters be trusted with larger responsibility?

Some principals will find it insulting if the applicant addresses the salutation to "Mr." if the principal is known as "Dr." Aside from pride, principals recognize how easy it is to get these details right. A teacher simply needs to place a phone call to the school and inquire if the principal listed on the website will be the principal in the coming year and ask additional questions to verify the incidental details.

If applicants seek to personalize the cover letter to an employer, it demands that the applicant conduct some research about the school. Fortunately, school websites often have significant information for the teacher to review. Applicants should become familiar with the size, demographics, and current academic performance of the school before applying. Many schools post their current school improvement plans for the public to review.

A school improvement plan is a gold mine of information for applicants. The plan will undoubtedly include a summary of the current reality for the school as well as the actions and initiatives that they are seeking to implement to reach their defined goals.

Applicants should not attempt to restate facts about the school in the cover letter in a contrived way. Saying something like "I see from your website that you have a 62% free/reduced lunch rate" is an awkward statement to make to communicate to an employer that the applicant has done a bit of homework and is attempting to personalize the letter. Instead, knowledge of the school should be included to make a larger point about the applicant's ability to become part of the solution for the school.

An applicant may take the information about poverty and weave it into the following statement: "When students live in poverty, educators have an additional set of challenges to meet their needs. I am certain that your school is no exception to this considering you have 62% of your students coming from homes that struggle financially. I believe that my experiences working in a Title 1 elementary school has equipped me with the skills to bridge these challenges for young people."

When a principal reads the second narrative, she will likely recognize that the applicant has done some research about the school but keeps the focus on how the applicant may be a part of their solution. While personalized connections are important, they must be framed within the context of how the applicant should be considered for the vacancy.

Sometimes the connections are harder to make if the experiences of a student teacher do not match so easily with the vacant position. On these occasions, applicants must find the way their skill set could be seen to match the need of the school. Rather than a vacancy in a diverse school setting, suppose that the vacant position is in a wealthier school with only 23 percent poverty levels. Should the applicant concede that she may not have anything to offer this school?

Imagine if the applicant were to merge this seemingly mismatched skill set with the vacant position by saying:

> During my student teaching experience, I had the great fortune of working in a Title I middle school that had over 70 percent of its students coming from poverty. Although I recognize that the makeup of your school is quite different in this regard, I do believe that the experiences I have had thus far are very valuable to your school as well. When students come to school from homes that are struggling financially, an additional set of burdens are added to learning.
>
> Although your school does not have a high percentage of students living in poverty, you certainly have several students who come from this background. These students will be facing additional burdens regardless of whether most of their peers aren't. In fact, it could be argued that it is even more difficult to be a student living in poverty when you do not see others with similar life circumstances around you.
>
> For this reason, I believe that your students in poverty may be even more at-risk than students with the same socioeconomic needs in another school. Because I have focused my professional experiences helping these students, I believe I can provide some additional support that may not currently exist because it is not a characteristic shared by great numbers of students in your school. Students do best in school when they find a sense of community around them. It could be very difficult for students to find their place in a school where they may not see themselves in those around them. With my assistance, I believe we can offer additional support to these students.

The applicant in this scenario recognizes that her limited professional experiences occurred in an environment that is very different than the school that has a vacant position. She does not try to pretend that the experience mirrors exactly what the school needs but finds a sensible and powerful way to draw a connection between the two very different settings.

Principals will not expect to find teachers who have professional experiences that completely overlap their own need. Rather, they may likely embrace different skills sets if they are able to make a connection in seeing how unique skills may be put to use in a novel way. However, the applicant cannot afford to hope that the principal makes this connection. The applicant must make overt connections for the hiring team.

Creating an easy leap between the skills purported by a stranger in a cover letter is the task. The cover letter does not need to convince the employer to give the applicant the position. The intent is to survive the application process and get the opportunity to meet in person during an interview.

The first paragraph of the cover letter is where the applicant must make this connection. The focus should be an expression of general knowledge of the school with sensible connections that create common ground. After the first paragraph, the applicant should detail the qualities and experiences that make her a strong applicant for the vacant position.

Applicants must seek clarity in understanding the actual position that is open within the school. An elementary teacher should not state that she is interested in an elementary teaching position but should note that it is a vacant third-grade position that she seeks. Likewise, a secondary teacher should not say that he would like to apply for a science position. Rather, he should note that he seeks the vacant biology and physical science job. This attention to detail sends the message that the applicant is not interested in *any* position but is seeking *this* position.

The most important reason for writing a quality cover letter is to keep the applicant alive in the process to gain the opportunity to sit for an interview. However, prospective teachers should not resign their fate to the submission of their application. While student teachers need to be cautious, they should also seize the opportunity to meet the principal of the school before the interview decisions are made.

Prospective teachers should reach out to the clerical staff of a school to inquire if they can stop by the school and drop off paperwork to the principal. Through a casual exchange by telephone, the teacher should be able to ascertain a time when the principal would be in the building but not occupied with other matters.

Before-school supervision, lunch duty, and after-school bus duty is a prime opportunity when principals are busy with professional duties but are likely to be available to engage in casual conversation. Prospective teachers must show care that they do not command a great deal of the principal's time. Rather, the teacher should simply seek to meet the principal to enable the principal to put a face to the name when the application is ultimately reviewed.

Because school districts likely have an online process for submitting materials, teachers need to be prepared with a short script to explain why they are appearing in person. For example, a prospective teacher may say, "I just wanted to stop by the school today and save you the trouble of printing off my materials that I have submitted online. I have certainly complied with the district procedures to apply, but thought I'd take the opportunity to introduce myself to you in person. I very much look forward to the prospect of visiting with you further if I am offered an interview."

By prefacing the conversation in this way, it clearly frames the purpose for coming to visit and should keep the principal from feeling unnerved by an applicant showing up in person in advance of upcoming interviews.

Teachers should put together a concise packet of information including their cover letter, resume, and letters of recommendation. Ideally, this should be organized in a thin folder that is easy to carry and store. Handing a principal a thick, three-ring binder becomes a nuisance to handle in the casual sort of way the teacher is approaching the administrator.

The prospective teacher should keep the introduction brief. Principals can become wary if they feel like one potential applicant is gaining an unfair advantage in the process. Meeting a candidate in person to receive material and an introduction is not an unfair advantage but trying to secure a "preinterview" in the process is.

The teachers should read the nonverbal communication of the principal carefully. If the principal wants to engage in further conversation, the teacher should obviously seize the opportunity. However, the teacher should not seek to protract out the conversation.

Focusing the conversation on the students and the building layout makes for easy and light conversation. If the principal seems receptive, teachers can ask if they are able to give themselves a self-tour of the building. This will send a message that the applicant is interested in the school but is not seeking to occupy the principal's time.

If the teacher can tour the building, it presents a prime opportunity to engage with others in conversation. Ideally, the applicant will know which grade level will be vacant and may have the chance to visit with partner teachers about their sense of the perceived needs on their team and in the building.

This information can provide critical insights to the applicant. Of course, prospective teachers should keep the conversation light and not come across as pushy or overly inquisitive. The prospective teacher needs to be delicate in an attempt to glean information from the staff members in the school.

Through this process, a wealth of information can be gathered without too much prodding. Rather than trying to convince staff members of personal strengths, the prospective teacher should instead look for insight on the dynamics occurring in the school that could be helpful in an interview setting. What are the needs of the school? What gaps do they believe they have? What type of person do they believe they need? In what ways are they currently struggling?

When teachers understand these questions, they can present themselves as the answer to the problems that are plaguing the school. For example, a partner teacher may hint that the students coming up to them next year seem to present a behavioral challenge. The prospective teacher can file away that tidbit of information and be certain to stress her skills with classroom management in an interview.

The opportunity to meet in the school where prospective teachers would like to interview is a tremendous advantage, but it is also a delicate opportunity to make the proper kind of impression. If staff members are tuned into the hiring process, they are likely making instantaneous judgments about the applicant as she tours the building.

Applicants should be warm and friendly throughout the time spent in the building. Prospective teachers must be careful not to make the mistake of merely trying to endear themselves to the principal of the school. Many teachers looking for work in a school have been denied the opportunity simply because the applicant was less than cordial to the receptionist.

Strong principals pay very close attention to the way in which potential teachers treat others in their building. Imagine the following exchange between a principal and her secretary after a potential applicant comes to visit.

Secretary: Who was that young man who came to visit with you during lunch hour today?

Principal: His name was Marcus. He intends to apply for our vacant math position. Did you visit with him?

Secretary: Yeah, I did actually. He was very nice. He asked me a lot about my work and the school. He seemed genuinely interested.

Principal: Did he interact with anyone else?

Secretary: Funny you should ask. Brady got sent down to the office and was waiting outside your door. Marcus asked how he was doing, what grade he was in, and what he liked best about our school.

Principal: Uh oh. How did Brady react to that?

Secretary: Really well. I think he could tell that the guy was genuinely interested in what he had to say. I must tell you I was pretty impressed.

In this scenario, Marcus made a strong impression on the staff of the school simply by being engaged and polite. The principal undoubtedly began forming opinions about Marcus as they chatted in the lunchroom. However, principals often seek to understand the impression that an applicant makes upon others as well.

It is easy to imagine that the principal relies heavily upon her administrative assistant and is very protective of her. Knowing that an applicant shows respect and kindness to the people who will not be hiring for the position is very important to thoughtful principals.

The goal for the applicant during this site visit is to associate a personal experience with the paperwork that is submitted. When principals review applications, they are often met with pages of unfamiliar names. There is a distinct advantage to the applicant whose name jumps off of the list because the principal remembers the personal impression associated with an earlier visit.

Even a brief in-person encounter can bring a personal connection to an applicant's submission. At this point, the personal connection is not intended to secure the position. Rather, the focus of the effort is to become memorable enough to secure an interview.

Once the application is complete and without error and the applicant has hand-delivered a copy as a courtesy to the principal, the applicant has done everything within her control. At this point, she should repeat the entire process for all other schools of interest. The same care and attention to detail that was shown to the first application by personalizing the cover letter and meeting the principal should be extended to every application.

Chapter 9

Interview Preparation

As a student teacher begins the preparation process for a teaching interview, it is important to remember that the skills required to be an excellent teacher are entirely different from the skills required to conduct a strong interview. Some teachers have excellent teaching skills but are unable to communicate their talent in the forum of a professional interview. Others seem to have the ability to convince interview teams of their merits as teachers without having the actual teaching skill set to back up their promises.

Student teachers have spent several months honing their teaching skills to be prepared to enter the teaching profession. However, they must first convince a hiring team that they are the best fit for the position. In the brief window of time when teachers are hired each spring, student teachers must assemble the best of their thoughts and work and be able to present themselves to others in a compelling way.

Fortunately, even though the skills required to teach and those required to interview well are very different, they are skills that can be learned. If every task has a technique that can be practiced and learned, interviewing for teaching jobs is no different.

Prospective teachers must embrace the last bit of work ahead of them before they can enter the profession. Teachers rarely fall into a teaching job if they interview poorly. Student teachers must recall that getting a job is their current job. The same hard work and tenacity that teachers put into their classroom instruction must be channeled into their interview preparation efforts.

Teachers should begin their preparation by giving some consideration to whom will likely be serving on the interview team. It would be a mistake to assume that a principal typically hires new teachers in the absence of forming a hiring committee. This group can be comprised of a wide variety of individuals. The composition of the team matters greatly for the teacher applicant and considering the range of professionals in the room is very important.

Typically, a person being interviewed will not know who will be serving on the interview committee in advance of the interview. However, speculating on the range of roles in the room is a beneficial exercise. For example, suppose the team comprises the building principal, a district-level administrator, and a partner teacher. If a candidate were asked a question on the adopted state standards, the appropriate response from the interviewee should be shaped by the presence of a team that is more formal and hierarchical.

In contrast, imagine if the interview team was made up of the building principal, a partner teacher, a special education teacher, and a parent. The complexion of this team is quite distinct from the other and would demand an altered focus. If a question were posed about state standards, the applicant should shape the response to the audience. For this team, a response that discusses the importance of flexibility and responsiveness in students' repeated attempts to achieve a lofty target is likely the more desirable response.

The applicant should not *change* their answers in an interview depending upon the audience. Rather, the teacher should highlight aspects of their response that is most likely to resonate with the team members in the room. Considering the range of nuanced responses that should be given depending upon the audience takes careful thought and preparation. This is especially difficult because applicants will find out the team members' roles in the brief introductions just minutes before answering their questions.

In the fleeting moments of the group introductions, applicants must pay very close attention to the roles that each team member plays. Everyone is guilty of forgetting a person's name a few seconds after being introduced. Holding on to people's names and the roles people play is essential for a good interview. Writing down the team member's names and roles during introductions is an easy technique to keep track of those in the room.

Even though a wide range of individuals may make up the team, the principal is likely to retain the final word on who is hired. An often-repeated maxim of the school administrator notes that if the principal is responsible for the firing, she is also responsible for the hiring. This knowledge should keep the applicants grounded in their responses.

The teacher cannot be all things to everyone with each response that is offered. Care should be given to highlight the aspects of an answer that will speak to the needs of the entire team, but ultimately, the prospective teacher should be answering the questions with the principal in mind.

How is an applicant to know what kind of answer a team is looking for in an interview? Typically, hiring teams will use scripted questions to guide the interview. They may even have a scoring rubric or key terms highlighted that they are looking for in an applicant's response. This should not be surprising as there are expected responses that accompany any topic in education.

If the question focuses on classroom management, the team will be hoping to hear the applicant discuss the need to preserve the learning environment, the importance of a fair but firm response to misbehavior, and the promise that the teacher will welcome the student back into the learning community without holding a grudge.

When the applicant notes these important "look-fors," team members will make notes and scribe the catch phrases and buzz words that resonate with them. However, there is always a deeper factor in play that shapes the hiring team's opinion of an applicant. One underlying question is always at the forefront of every person's mind and forms their judgment despite any answers that are offered.

Will this person make my life easier or harder? This question sneaks into the subconscious of even the most dedicated and objective hiring team member. That is not to say that the question is as superficial and selfish as it may appear at first blush. Certainly, team members sometimes form opinions for less than noble reasons. Many weak teachers have secured their positions simply because the hiring team was less threatened by them than a better, more assertive applicant who may have challenged her peers' practices.

Aside from those occasion, the question of whether an applicant will make others' lives easier or harder is not entirely inappropriate. Rather, it is a stripped-down way for people to form a judgment about another as they are being barraged with information and responses in a short period of time.

In the following scenario, a teacher is asked a question about how he might handle a student who has repeated, explosive behavior issues in class. The interview team is composed of the principal, a partner teacher, a parent, and a special education teacher.

Principal: Please describe for us how you might handle a student who exhibits repeated and explosive behaviors in your class?

Applicant: Well, maintaining an appropriate learning environment for all students is my primary concern. Students must feel safe if they are going to learn. I would involve the principal and any available counseling staff to discuss the issue with the parents to see what we could do to improve the behavior.

In response to the answer, the team member would certainly be jotting notes like: "maintain the learning environment," "students must feel safe," and "involve others." While the applicant may not have said anything wrong by giving this response, it is worth noting the likely conversations going on in the heads of each team member in that moment.

Principal: Is he going to turn this entire issue over to me? I wonder if he will bring every single misbehavior to me to resolve? Does he understand the importance of progressive discipline? Am I going to have an office full of students because they forgot to bring their pencil to class?

Partner teacher: Oh great. He's going to use the sanctity of the learning environment response as a reason to dump kids out of his classroom. I guess that means I will be getting every single student who has a behavioral problem if we hire this guy.

Parent: I appreciate that he wants to keep my child safe and focused on learning. It is such a breath of fresh air to hear a teacher acknowledge the rights that other students have to learn without being continually interrupted and scared by other kids who can't control themselves.

Special Education teacher: I wonder if this teacher has any training with behavioral supports for students? I guess I appreciate he will involve others but I wonder if that means asking them for help or trying to off-load this student for others to manage?

What began as a reasonable answer by the applicant has spun completely out of control in the minds of the hiring team. Because the teacher failed to discuss intermediate measures as a response to poor behavior, the principal is assuming that the teacher would abandon all responsibility for working with students when they misbehave. The teacher certainly did not say this, but the teacher's silence on that aspect of the question will be replaced with uncertainty on the part of the principal.

Likewise, the partner teacher is left with many unresolved concerns. Because the teacher chose to emphasize the importance of preserving the educational environment without considering the perceived fallout on the other end, the partner teacher is suspicious of the teacher's beliefs about taking responsibility for highly troubled students. This may not be the belief of the applicant, but silence on the issue causes questions to remain.

The parent's response to the teacher's comment reveals the complexity of interviewing with diverse hiring committees. This parent loved the teacher's response and was encouraged that someone in the system is finally acknowledging the importance of the common good when classrooms are disrupted. This parent is focused primarily on the experience of her child and is completely satisfied with the candidate's answer.

The special education teacher is left somewhere between all the others. She is pleased that she is recognized as a valuable resource on the staff but is uncertain of whether the teacher wishes to form a true partnership in the work. While this teacher would not likely have a bad impression of the candidate based on the response, she is likely nervous about bringing the teacher on board without further evidence to reassure her of his competency.

Each member of a hiring team plays an integral role in the functioning of the school system. The special education teacher has not been tasked with considering how difficult the principal's job may be. She has plenty of responsibilities of her own. Because of this, each of them listens to a candidate's response and wonders whether that person will make life easier or harder. Trying to answer difficult questions while acknowledging these related, but distinct, interests is not easy.

Because of the complexity that these considerations pose, the teacher candidate must engage in a significant amount of preparation work in advance. It is difficult to compose an adequate answer to difficult professional questions. It is even more challenging to consider how different professionals might interpret each response.

Although the exact composition of the hiring team may not be announced beforehand, an applicant certainly can inquire if that information is available. Because it is a question that can seem a bit presumptuous to ask, an applicant should be discreet in inquiring. One useful tactic is to call the administrative assistant to the principal and say, "I would like to prepare materials to hand out in the interview, can you let me know the number of people who will be on the hiring team so I can make sure I have enough?"

This question is certainly reasonable and will not be met with suspicion. Upon hearing the number on the team, it is more natural to follow up with the question, "Am I able to know the different roles of those on the team so I can make sure I include all appropriate attachments?" Because the applicant did not press for actual names of the committee members, an administrative assistant may be likely to pass along the information as it is couched as a legitimate inquiry in the applicant's attempt to prepare materials for the interview. Obviously, if a school is not willing to divulge the information, there is nothing lost by inquiring.

If a candidate knows the roles of the committee members, visualizing the way the interview should proceed is much easier. The candidate can imagine the best ways to answer questions considering their respective roles. Also, there is an opportunity to play devil's advocate in considering what kinds of things each person would and would not hope to hear in the answer. Preparing in this way ensures that the candidate does not fail to address an important aspect of the question.

If the applicant is not able to know which roles will be represented on the committee, it is often helpful simply to know the number of people on the hiring team. If an applicant is told that there will be three people on the team, there will be a much more intimate and personal interview environment. If, by contrast, there are ten members of the hiring team, the applicant will also know that there will be a wide variety of roles represented and, by virtue of the sheer numbers, the environment will be far less personal and intimate.

Before considering the actual questions that may be asked, the applicant should invest more time in becoming very familiar with the school. How do you pronounce the principal's name? Does the principal go by Ms., Mrs., or

Dr.? What is the school mascot? What are the school colors? Am I clear on what grades the building serves? Do I know the demographics?

This preparation work should not be done so the applicant presents herself as an expert regarding the school. Hiring committees are very sensitive to those who seem to have all the answers when they have never stepped into the building. Rather than pretending to have expertise regarding the school, applicants should use the knowledge they have gained as reference points in answering questions.

For example, if the hiring committee asks a question about the importance of forming strong relationships with students, there are two very different responses a teacher may provide:

Applicant #1: Forming strong relationships with students is very important to me. I believe you can do that by showing interest in their lives and asking them about their passions.

Applicant #2: Developing strong relationships with students is indeed important but relationships must be rooted in strong connections with students. One way I would do that is to introduce myself by sending home a welcome back letter to all families asking if they are coming to the back to school barbecue I noticed you have advertised for the second week of August. I'd also become involved in the things that are important to them. For example, I would join the kids in the Commons where I know the Chess Club meets every morning, and I'd be in the stands cheering for the Vikings in their home opener against the Broncs. Strong relationships are formed with shared experiences, and I'm committed to being a part of my students' lives.

The second applicant has done her research. However, she didn't use her knowledge to list the things she knows about the school to prove the point she knows random facts about the school. Instead, she uses her research to add color and description to the way in which she would connect with students. In truth, all she really knew was that there is a back-to-school barbecue planned, the school has a Chess Club that meets in the mornings, and the school mascot is the Vikings.

This teacher weaves those three pieces of trivia together to paint a picture. With one response, the hiring team will picture her in the stands wearing black and gold, cheering for *her* kids. The team is already envisioning her as a teacher in their school simply because she engaged in a bit of homework.

In addition to gleaning information about the possible interview committee and conducting some background research on the school, teacher candidates must also consider how able they are to connect with others in a professional conversation. Because teacher candidates are coming straight from the collegiate environment (and may also be quite young), they are faced with both the challenge of engaging in a professional conversation with highly trained educators and the task of bridging possible generation gaps with those whom they will be meeting.

Typically, school principals tend to be in touch with the younger generation because they spend so much time interacting with kids. However, that does not mean that there will not be a significant generation gap between an applicant and the principal of a school. Although principals are usually connected with youth, they do not desire their new teacher to remind them of their students.

Principals need to be reassured that the person interviewing with them is a highly trained professional. Because teachers entering the profession have not yet functioned as a teacher in a full-time capacity, a gap exists. This gap that exists must be bridged, and it is entirely the job of the applicant to bridge this gap.

Like it or not, teachers do not get to hire themselves. Regardless of the qualifications and abilities of teachers, a principal must decide to invest in them by offering them a position. Likely, one person has been entrusted to confirm all the hiring for the entire organization. This creates a very narrow gate through which all prospective teachers need to pass. The principal in this regard is the gatekeeper.

How then does a person new to the profession bridge these gaps to enter through the narrow gate of professional scrutiny? Potential teachers must recognize that the principals hiring them are much older, and they likely view the world through a different generational lens. This lens includes some preconceived notions of bad habits that typify the stereotypes of younger generations.

Of course, any given individual may not have the traits that are associated with his particular generation. However, an applicant desiring employment should take great care to understand the undesirable traits that give administrators caution in hiring new people.

For example, much has been made of the personality characteristic of young professionals who have embraced the flexibility that working remotely has brought to modern life. Because of the constant connectivity and availability, many young people have not lived their lives in a way where their physical presence is needed at a specific time and place.

Obviously, schools do not operate in this fashion. Every day, school will begin at a predetermined time with the ringing of the school bell and a classroom full of young students ready to begin their instruction. Because of this fact, it is never acceptable for a teacher to be running late to work. Tardiness for teachers is simply unacceptable. If a young person has grown accustomed to the flexibility of a work environment where time is made up on the end of the day if a worker is late to arrive, it simply cannot be accommodated in a school setting. This generational tendency has no place in a public school classroom.

In the same way, much has been made of the decreasing attention spans that young people have acquired due to the constant stimulation of the electronic world. This is also a habit that may need to be broken for a new employee. If a newly hired teacher has developed a tendency to check social media throughout the day, there is no acceptable place for that kind of distraction from the daily obligations of a teacher.

Prospective teachers must also conduct a self-audit of their current online footprint. As a matter of due diligence, most principals make a regular habit of conducting Internet searches of their teacher candidates. The way in which teachers present themselves on social media can cause sufficient concern for a principal to screen out an applicant on that basis alone. Prospective teachers should be mindful that principals do not owe an applicant an interview. If principals are indeed tasked with sorting out who they do not want for a job before they select a few to interview, a questionable social media presence can immediately end an applicant's chances.

For example, if an applicant has pictures posted that highlight drinking or wearing swimsuits or suggestive clothing, the principal may be alarmed. Aside from the generation gap where an older administrator cannot fathom the poor judgment in releasing intimate or compromising pictures, the principal is likely to note that young children could just as easily view the pictures and see their teacher engaged in questionable behavior.

Likewise, prospective teachers should audit their own online postings of questionable written comments as well. Many teaching careers have been prematurely ended by posting inflammatory or vulgar topics for public viewing. If a principal sees that a prospective teacher uses profanity in a public venue, that principal is likely going to keep searching the pile of applications for someone who doesn't.

The personal habits that one acquires over time can follow patterns of a larger group or can be highly personalized. Either way, teaching candidates need to reflect upon their own behaviors with great scrutiny to ensure that some of their hardwired actions are not impeding their ability to be employable. The hierarchy of authority and accompanying expectations for schools does not always lend itself to self-expression. Teachers must consider how they must adapt their tendencies if they want to be a part of the profession.

The language of the workplace (and certainly the language of a job interview) is a more formal register than normal, casual conversation. If a prospective teacher is unaccustomed to engaging in the style of speech that is customary in the workplace, she must begin practicing that voice immediately. It is important to note that the professional voice is distinct from the voice a teacher uses in the classroom. While there is an obvious expectation that student teachers behave in a professional manner around students, it is likely a voice that students find comfortable. When new teachers begin interacting with colleagues and their superiors, they must take great care to utilize a voice that is appropriate for a professional setting.

The first opportunity teachers will have to engage in this professional dialogue is in the interview process. Teachers should take care to find a voice that is warm and friendly, but one that is not too casual for the occasion. Applicants should reflect on their typical manner of speech and determine if they are prone to using slang or lazy contractions ("I was tryin' to finish my degree early."). Depending on each person's tendencies, the amount of focus and practice that will be required to engage in professional conversation that is not stilted or awkward will vary.

The best method to assess the way in which candidates appear in this formal setting is to video themselves in a mock interview. With a quick Internet search, a teacher can find several sample interview questions for teachers. If the prospective teacher is too shy to ask a friend to conduct the mock interview, the teacher can read a question off the list and then respond to it as if it were posed in an actual interview setting.

There are a few things a person should look for when reviewing video of a mock interview. Before critiquing the answers to the questions, the teacher candidate should evaluate things such as posture, mannerisms, eye contact, rate of speech, and the proper use and enunciation of words. Viewing oneself on video can be a very revealing exercise that will surely bring embarrassment in the beginning. Rarely do people see themselves performing in a professional manner and the initial results, while beneficial, can be quite shocking.

Rather than completing an entire battery of interview questions, a teacher should answer and review the footage in small chunks. This will make the task more manageable and ensure that mistakes are not being rehearsed and practiced, but rather identified and eliminated.

Although the Internet may provide a rich source of potential interview questions, a prospective teacher can anticipate likely interview questions to a greater degree than is typically realized. To begin the work of prepping responses for specific questions, the teacher should refer to their professional portfolio. Not only will the resources in the portfolio provide the raw material in constructing powerful answers, but it can also provide some guidance on potential questions as well.

Interview candidates should remember that the hiring team can ask only a small number of questions. Because a typical interview is likely to be limited to an hour, candidates can usually expect ten to fifteen questions as the basis for their interview. Considering the wide variety of topics in education that are important to consider, teams will not likely ask redundant questions on the same topic.

If a teacher refers to the evaluation instrument as the basis for a comprehensive description of the wide range of duties for a teacher, it also provides the basis for the variety of topics that the teacher will likely be asked in an interview. Applicants should make a bulleted list of general areas of responsibility such as lesson planning, assessment of student work, communication with families, and classroom management. This list should include every category within the evaluation rubric. Certainly, some hiring teams may not ask a specific question on every topic, but the candidate should be prepared to do so.

For each identified category, the teacher should make a bulleted list underneath highlighting important points for each. The teacher should be wary against cluttering up the page with words so obvious that they aren't worth mentioning. For example, for the category of classroom management, it would be beneficial to include a bullet point that says, "progressive discipline." By contrast, including the word "important" or "necessary" is not very helpful. Words that an interviewee would be sure to say without the reminder of the list should not be included.

For every category, teachers should also include either the reference to an artifact collected during the student teaching experience or an anecdotal story relating to that category. The bulleted list for each category should be relatively short. As a teacher prepares thoughts for each category, it is important to remember that the candidate should not spend more than three to four minutes for each response.

Because of the need to be succinct, the very important stories that an interview candidate needs to tell must be streamlined and pared down to the degree that it can serve the purpose of quickly making the desired point without dragging out and taking up too much time.

Some academic preparation programs suggest that students put together a beliefs matrix to distribute to members of a hiring team. The problem with listing valued beliefs in a matrix with bulleted descriptors is that it tends to be very general and nonpersonalized. Sharing a matrix with an employer that highlights valuable traits such as work ethic, flexibility, and lifelong learning seems entirely reasonable. However, one cannot imagine that any candidate would offer the alternative to these qualities. Lazy, rigid, and close-minded would never be the substance of a rational person's list.

Because of these natural similarities, there tends to be very little difference between what any candidate may supply. Therefore, offering a beliefs matrix for a hiring team to review may not be very useful. Instead, producing a matrix for each expected category of possible question as a resource for the applicant to use during the interview is far more logical.

Hiring teams would not be surprised if an applicant opened a folder during the interview to jot down notes and refer to the reference sheet discreetly as the interview progresses. However, teachers being interviewed should have sufficient command of the document that they rarely need to look at it. Instead, it can serve as a gentle reminder for teachers if their nerves get the best of them and they get lost in their thoughts and need to get recentered in their answers.

Aside from notes about every important category of possible questions that may be asked, preparation should also include a review of the professional portfolio to decide which pieces of student work best represent the teacher's skills and could be referenced at the appropriate time in the interview. If the applicant wants to share any documents with all the team members, she should not leave any materials for the team to review that must be returned. To leave a hiring team with documents to review is to create a pile of homework for them to work through. Because the team is interviewing several candidates, they will not have the time to give materials further review.

Instead, the applicant should provide copies of documents only for providing a visual aid during the interview. Referring to a document as a question is being answered can be a powerful way to answer a question. However, candidates should refrain from handing out any documents that do not advance an answer to a specific question.

One of the greatest challenges for new teacher candidates is creating a noticeable level of distinction between themselves and other candidates. The reality is that new teachers typically have very similar life experiences and training. Every candidate has recently finished a college preparatory program. Candidates also share very similar student teaching experiences and likely have a short list of volunteer work and experiences.

The good news is that hiring teams are not surprised that new teachers lack substantial experience. However, teams are looking for any indications of superior preparation or experiences. This is the reason why vivid stories and gathered student artifacts serve such an important purpose.

Prospective teachers are faced with the challenge of expressing their uniqueness to the hiring committee. Unfortunately, candidates cannot hope to rely on the interview questions to reveal what is best about them. The questions a team chooses may not automatically elicit responses from a candidate that demonstrate true distinction among those being interviewed. Therefore, it is incumbent upon the teacher being interviewed to help the team come to believe in their strengths and skills that set them apart from the crowd.

Teachers can do this by creating a list of five qualities that make them truly special. Everyone has a particular mix of strengths that make them unique. These are the skills that others seem to point out as compliments. Teachers should reflect on the five best qualities about themselves and determine when and how they will work those traits into their responses during the interview.

For example, if a teacher has a strong work ethic, that quality must be highlighted. A candidate for hire cannot hope that the team will ask a specific question about work ethic. Instead, the teacher could work this characteristic into the conversation in the following way:

Committee member: Please discuss the importance of formative assessment in student learning.

Teacher: There are many different types of formative assessment depending on how formal the teacher desires to collect information. At times, it can be as simple as having students give a thumbs up or a thumbs down as a response. The key to formative assessment is how you intend to change instruction considering the information you have gathered. I like to conduct more formalized formative assessments as well. Of course, the stakes are still low for students as they are early in the instructional process, but I like to ask my students to complete exit slips when they leave class each day. These exit slips briefly assess their mastery of the learning target for the day. Each day, I come in to school at 6:00 a.m. and review the exit slips from the prior day. This helps me to make new decisions on re-teaching certain topics or regrouping students in the upcoming day's instruction.

With this response, the teacher has demonstrated several important ideas. Primarily, the question was about formative assessment. She needed to answer that well by demonstrating her understanding of the importance of formative assessment and did so by giving specific examples.

However, the teacher also left the team with a strong impression of her work ethic. One can imagine the team thinking, "She comes in at 6:00 every day? She produces exit slips daily?" The teacher wanted to impart her strong work ethic to the committee and found a way to do so without announcing it directly. Teams are not as likely to be impressed by a teacher claiming to possess a strong quality as they are if the picture is painted of that quality in action. Regardless of the questions asked, teachers must work their five most prized traits into the conversation.

A teacher must commit to a significant amount of preparation in advance of the interview. As difficult as the commitment of time and effort may be, it is a worthy short-term investment with a significant long-term payoff. The interview itself will likely cause great nervousness for a teacher candidate. The best way to reduce anxiety and nervousness is to be very well prepared. The short window of time between finishing student teaching and interviewing for vacant positions provides a sufficient span of time if the teacher chooses to seize the occasion.

Chapter 10

Mastering the Interview

The interview begins the minute a candidate walks through the doors. All eyes will be upon the candidate noting mannerisms, disposition, and affect toward others. Because the candidate will likely be quite nervous, it is important that the interviewee does not become so preoccupied that he fails to greet and thank everyone upon entering the building.

Everything about the prospective teacher will be used as evidence for or against the teacher throughout the process. The first impression will certainly be a visual one. The clothing and appearance of the applicant will be the first test upon arrival. It is important to remember that teaching is a highly social profession and appearances matter greatly.

Potential teachers must make a financial investment in themselves and purchase clothes suitable for a job interview. As a society, people have become far more casual in their appearance in many different aspects of life. A generation or two ago, people got dressed up to take a flight on an airplane or to attend a sporting event. In those days, it was not uncommon to see business clothes as the standard gear.

These days, it's hard to find an occasion that warrants dress clothes. Indeed, many people simply do not own them. This presents an odd contrast. The young man who clears the table at a chain restaurant may likely wear a shirt and tie as part of the dress code, but someone who works in an office building may wear jeans to work. The service industry continues to value professional attire, while many businesses do not.

This is certainly true in education as well. Many teachers are allowed to dress in ways that hardly distinguish them from the students they serve. While this may be unfortunately true for those who already have a job, those seeking a job simply cannot approach the interview in anything less than professional attire. If a principal is watching a group of three men visiting in the distance who are gathered for interviews at a job fair, she will undoubtedly have different impressions if one is dressed in a polo shirt and khakis, another is wearing a shirt and tie, and the third is wearing a suit. Before hearing any of them speak, she is likely to have a more favorable impression of the man in a suit. He already possesses a distinct advantage.

In a similar way, women need to be careful in choosing appropriate attire for an interview. Business clothes are a must, but even these come in a wide range of styles. Women should strive to find a look that is tasteful and classy. Great care should be taken against wearing clothes that are revealing or too tight. There is certainly a way to retain a look of femininity without looking provocative. Anything that pushes the boundaries in this regard is likely to make a hiring team too uncomfortable to consider the merits of what a candidate is saying.

Perhaps there was a time when it could be argued that dress clothes were too expensive for a college student struggling financially. This is no longer the case. An interviewee can find acceptable dress clothes for far less than the price of some designer jeans on the shelves. The potential teacher cannot think of the investment in terms of whether he is likely to wear the suit very often after securing a position. Wearing anything less than a suit diminishes the chance of securing the position to the point it should not even be a consideration.

Of course, clothes are the first consideration teachers should have in making sure their looks are pulled together in a professional manner. Teachers should also consider their personal hygiene from the perspective of a hiring team passing collective judgment on applicants. Potential teachers should consider the way in which styles and trends may work against them in the professional interview setting.

For example, it is not uncommon to see a man in public with an unshaven face exposing a few days of whisker growth. This is far from being socially unacceptable. However, on the day of a job interview, trendiness could easily be mistaken for sloppiness.

Likewise, some women choose to paint their finger nails. There is certainly nothing troubling about that trend. However, after a few days, finger nail polish tends to chip away. Both painted and unpainted finger nails look professional, but chipped finger nail polish is more reminiscent of a ten-year-old than a dedicated professional. *Might chipped finger nail polish really make a candidate lose the job?* Perhaps it wouldn't, but a principal distracted by the sloppiness will mean that she is paying less attention to the candidate's answers than to her fingers. Distracting the team's focus in any way is a mistake.

Many people may take issue with others dictating matters of style and appearance. Certainly, a principal would have no input or opinion on how teachers look when they are eating at a local restaurant. However, administrators often weigh in heavily on the issue of teacher appearance in the workplace.

It cannot be stressed enough that teachers will have to meet expectations of dress daily, but they have an even more critical expectation on the day of the interview. By federal law, hiring teams cannot discriminate based on protected classes. Candidates are assured that issues surrounding their race, age, and sex will not be the basis for hiring decisions. However, matters of personal taste and preference are not protected classes.

If a candidate chooses to dye her hair green, that boldness must be matched with the realization that hiring teams may not be impressed. If a candidate prefers to wear ten articles of jewelry as a fashion statement, it runs the risk of teams being distracted. If a candidate chooses to have multiple piercings in his face, principals may find it off-putting enough to look elsewhere to fill the position.

Matters of personal style and trendiness may likely present a larger generation gap than manners of speaking or attitudes. How people choose to present themselves physically usually produces a quicker and more visceral reaction. Indeed, a candidate may be able to make either a very positive or very negative reaction before even speaking a word. In the same way that a woman wears a different face in her role as daughter, wife, or classical pianist, the role of teacher has certain expectations as well. If a candidate truly wants the job, these details cannot be overlooked.

One way for teachers to demonstrate a subtle sign of respect in their attire is to coordinate their outfit with the colors of the school. This is an easy way to make an immediate connection with the school personnel reminding them that the candidate is tuned into the school culture and would like to become a part of it.

Upon entering the school and certainly the interview room, the interviewee should introduce herself, shake hands, and smile at every person she meets. As the school personnel debrief after the interview, a candidate will regret if one person responds by saying, "Well, I must not be important enough in her eyes to even say hello." Even if everyone else in the room is impressed with this potential teacher, perceived rudeness is difficult to overcome and may end with a fatal result.

Because of the tension associated with the occasion, it is easy for an interviewee to forget to smile. Even if it requires that the teacher prompt herself in her notes to smile at different points in the interview, she should do so. Similarly, maintaining eye contact in stressful moments is not easy either. Some find eye contact difficult even under casual circumstances. However, eye contact is an easy way to create the highly personalized experience that the teacher desperately needs. If the teacher being interviewed finds this difficult to maintain, she should fix her attention in the center of the forehead of the person to whom she is speaking. This lessens the forced intimacy of the moment but is not a noticeable tactic to the recipient.

Of course, even though a teacher may need to remind herself to smile and greet others warmly, this must be met with balance. The power of being personable is in its subtlety. The candidate should not be overly dramatic and gush when meeting the people in the room. The friendliness should be ever-present but not over the top.

The candidate must remember that hiring teams are fundamentally looking for a good person. They may certainly want more than a good person, but they will never settle for a person with weak social skills if possible. Smiling and maintaining eye contact sends strong unconscious messages to the team that the candidate is warm and caring. The team will believe these traits are genuine when they *feel* them, not when they *hear* them.

For these reasons, a candidate should not conduct an interview remotely if possible. Many candidates have purchased a plane ticket to interview in person with little more than a one-hour interview slot as a promise of what may come. It is doubtful that a hiring committee would select against a candidate because they conducted a phone interview. However, all the affective skills that a candidate possesses that are at the heart of what the committee is seeking are absent.

An interview is more than just the sum of the things that the teaching candidate says. Rather, it is a complete package of demeanor, attitude, and enthusiasm that play out in the answers that a candidate gives. This is nearly impossible to communicate if the candidate is not interacting with the team in person.

Aside from the interpersonal communication gaps that are created because of a remote interview, a teacher should also be cautious of pursuing a job in a school and community that is unknown. A school always has a different feel than the way it is described on the website. Personally witnessing the dynamics and nuances of a place is important. After all, even though a prospective teacher is working hard to get a job, meeting the administrator and coworkers within the actual teaching environment may matter enough to sway a decision if the job were offered.

As the interviewee begins the actual interview, she will undoubtedly be quite nervous. Not only does the interview present incredibly high stakes professionally for the teacher, but it is also a stressful environment that is mostly foreign to the new teacher. The reality is that most people have very little experience of being interviewed. Ironically, those with the most experience are candidates who have had the least amount of success in securing a position. Some veteran teachers in the field of education have been through the interview process only one time.

The teacher being interviewed should not believe that the nervousness will be wished away in the moment. Likely, she will be nervous from the very beginning and will remain nervous throughout. However, there is an excellent technique to mitigate the nervousness of the moment.

During the initial introductions of the interviewee and the team when everybody is getting settled, there is usually some light conversation as everyone is getting seated. The principal is likely to tell the teacher where to sit and ask how her morning is progressing. During this informal exchange as the principal is introducing the candidate to each member of the team, there is likely a brief window of opportunity for the teacher to greet the team as a collective unit.

If the candidate is experiencing a level of nervousness that makes her believe her nerves may be noticeable and affect her answers, she could say, "I must admit that I am very nervous right now. Although that should not be surprising, I suppose, as we all get nervous about things in life that are very important to us. I hope you'll forgive me if it is noticeable."

This sort of response acknowledges the elephant in the room. If a teacher tries to hide her nervousness, she is likely to get even more nervous as she stumbles upon her words or feels her voice quivering. Every person in the interview room will remember their own nervousness when they secured their first position and will be immediately sympathetic. This sort of honesty does not expose a weakness; it validates the humanness of the candidate. This is a sort of relatedness that actually builds the relationship.

As the teacher settles in to begin the formal interview, the principal may give detailed information about how the interview will proceed. Sometimes, the principal will give the interviewee a copy of the questions in order for the teacher to follow along. At other times, the principal may not give any information and simply launch into the scripted questions.

If the principal does not provide any details before beginning the interview, the teacher should ask the following question, "Am I able to know how many questions you have prepared and how long we are scheduled so I can be sure to budget my time accordingly?" A question like this is certainly fair game and will not be a complete surprise to the team.

Based on the answer that the principal gives, the teacher should quickly calculate how many minutes she is able to afford to spend on any given question. This is crucial because of the tendency for teachers to underestimate the importance of timing. This can hurt a teacher on both ends of the spectrum. Many teachers have walked away from an interview after leaving a half hour unused because they sped through the questions too quickly. This is most unfortunate as the teacher preempted her own efforts to paint a picture of her talents.

Teachers can also be at risk of trying to say too much in any given question. In these cases, a teacher provides far too much detail and then limits her ability to give a thorough answer later in the interview. Because hiring teams recognize the importance of giving every applicant the same interview experience, teachers can expect to be cut off when the time limit expires whether they have even attempted to answer some of the questions. After all, it wouldn't be fair to cut into another applicant's interview time by giving a prior candidate more time and opportunity to compete for the position.

Aside from budgeting time wisely, prospective teachers can also run the risk trying to answer every possible question with any given question. Consider the following scenario where a hiring team begins the interview with an introductory question:

> *Principal*: Please tell us about your educational background and experiences that would make you a good fit for the position.
>
> *Teacher*: I am graduating this spring with a degree in secondary English. I have completed the process for licensure and will be endorsed to teach every course you offer in your building. I did my student teaching across town at Evans Junior High school. It was an incredible experience.
>
> As a student teacher I taught with Ms. Kincaid and taught four sections of seventh-grade English and two sections of eighth-grade English. I met weekly in their collaborative team and learned a lot about teamwork. We also did some very interesting work with developing assessments that mirror the state exam. We worked in our team developing a procedure for inter-rater reliability, so we can be sure to assess every student in a fair and consistent way.

The teacher began her answer in a completely acceptable manner. She detailed her coursework and provided very pertinent information about the nature of her degree and the kinds of courses she is certified to teach. At this point, however, she attempts to jam too much information into the actual question that was asked.

It is quite likely that the team would devote a question to the importance of teamwork and collaboration. She had a good experience in this area and wants to make sure she introduces it into the conversation. However, it goes far beyond the actual question asked. Likewise, her experience with developing assessments and building a strong system of quality control around the process is quite noteworthy. This experience deserves to be a part of the conversation, but she would be better off waiting for a question on assessments to do so.

Aside from cluttering her answers with too much information, she also missed out on an opportunity to answer the question they posed in a more comprehensive manner. A question about background is a prime opportunity to make connections with the team. She could have mentioned the university where she received her degree. Perhaps others on the team went to the same school. Likewise, the candidate may have had some experiences that would not naturally come up in another question.

For example, if the candidate had done some volunteer work, this was the time to discuss it. It is unlikely that the team would devote an entire question to such a topic. This was the question where she had the opportunity to elaborate on her own resume that would make her a unique and special fit for their school. Instead of relaying the opportunities she was able to observe during her student teaching experience, she could have seized the chance to paint a highly personalized picture of her unique attributes and qualifications. This was a question meant to figure out who she is, not what she witnessed.

Prospective teachers can also make the mistake of veering off the target question and begin answering a different (unasked) question. In the following example, the teacher is asked a question about the importance of teamwork:

Principal: Could you describe for us how you would function as a team member in our school with other teachers?

Teacher: Teamwork is so important. Long gone are the days where teachers can function as independent contractors within a school. I have a lot of experience working in a collaborative team. During my student teaching, we met every day for a half hour looking at student work. It was very exciting because we were able to understand specific skill gaps students had. Based on those skill gaps, students were placed in appropriate interventions.

Some of the options we had were second immersion experiences during tier one instruction time where students received more practice on the skills they needed to improve. However, it also revealed that some students needed more intensive interventions and we were able to set aside some time during the day for a block of intervention time. These students met with our full-time interventionist and received individualized attention. We also had an extended day program where students could get tutoring after their school day had ended to receive more assistance. I think it worked out really well, and we saw a lot of students make significant academic gains.

The teacher being interviewed started off strong in her answer acknowledging the importance of teamwork in a school setting. However, she began to lose her way when she started describing the work of her team. In an attempt to be thorough, she proceeded to explain the intervention options for her students in great detail.

While she may have impressed the team on her understanding of thoughtful interventions for students, she did not actually answer the question about the role she plays within her collaborative team. Because of the way in which she answered the question, she failed to give examples of how she personally contributed to the team. Has she ever taken the lead within the group? How does she contribute her own thoughts when they may be different than the prevailing will of the group? Has she ever helped another teacher who was struggling to find his voice on the team?

These are the answers the team hoped to hear when they asked the question. If the earlier example portrayed the danger of fitting too much in to a single question, this example demonstrates the problem of answering a question that was not asked. It is important to remember that the team purposefully posed specific questions. They are looking for answers to the chosen questions. The team is not interested in simply listening to the candidate speak for an hour. Rather, they want to hear the interviewee's thoughts on the specific questions they chose.

Teachers must not be content with simply filling time in the interview with their responses. The answers a teacher gives must be a thoughtful and targeted response to build the case to be hired. The teacher is not providing answers as much as she is convincing the team that she is their answer. Every response makes a deposit into the account. The sum of those deposits will result in the hiring team recognizing that the teacher has made a sufficient investment that the choice is obvious.

Teachers do not fail to answer questions properly or veer off topic on accident. Sometimes, they can be drawn into a dead-end path by the interview team. As a teacher begins to respond to a question, she should be maintaining eye contact with the members of the team as she answers. For their part, the team members will often return the gaze and may begin to respond in several nonverbal ways.

For example, when a teacher supplies an answer to a question, team members will often smile and nod their head slightly. Usually, this is nothing more than a way for a team member to respond in a polite way rather than showing agreement to the answers the teacher is giving. Teachers need to be cautious when recognizing these nonverbal signals. Often, teachers feel emboldened by the support they interpret they are receiving and will continue to reinforce the point that has garnered such a positive response.

In these moments, teachers can lose sight of the answer they intended to give and end up misusing their limited time by adding emphasis and detail to a good point they have already made. Teachers can also fall into this trap when committee members begin scribbling down notes in response to the things that the interviewee says.

Committee members feel compelled to jot down notes during an interview. Not only is it a way to capture important ideas that are shared, but it is also a natural way for the committee to stay engaged with the process. Teachers may be a bit surprised to read the actual notes that a committee member writes down. Often, it will not always be the most important points that have been made. Rather, it can simply be the easiest phrases to capture in the moment.

Teachers should not read too much into the writing (or lack thereof) of the committee members. Certainly, teachers should not modify or extend their answers in response to the frequency of the committee members' note-taking. Teachers need to focus on giving the best response they can and not look for affirmation in the moment.

Interviewees can also misinterpret facial expressions of committee members during an interview. Committee members are not likely focusing on their own poker face during an interview and may exhibit a wide range of emotions on their faces and in their body language.

For example, when a teacher is responding to a question, a principal may furrow his brow in response. In that moment, the teacher may assume that the principal does not like the answer and begin revising her thoughts. This can be a very big mistake. People furrow their brows for a wide variety of reasons. Perhaps the principal heard a very intriguing response and is wondering why he has never thought of that idea before. In this case, a furrowed brow is a very promising piece of feedback. However, the teacher will never be able to know in that moment.

Sometimes, a principal may react emotionally because of the strong truth of the message that the teacher is sending. As a result, the principal may have a look of disappointment on his face because he realizes his school is currently not performing in the way that the teacher is describing. Because it is so difficult to discern what the principal may be thinking, the teacher should not attempt to decipher the hidden messages.

The messages extend to body language as well. A committee member may lean forward or back in a chair simply to shift body weight rather than showing a response to what is being said. Ultimately, people send a wide range of signals with the same few behaviors. As such, a teacher cannot be distracted from the movements of the committee members throughout the interview.

Considering all the suggestions concerning what a teacher should not do, it can become difficult to sort through all of the advice and decide what exactly needs to be said in an interview. This is vitally important. It is not enough to recognize the warning signs of how an interview can go wrong, but it is a completely different proposition in knowing how to proceed to be successful.

Above all, a prospective teacher needs to take a genuine and honest approach to the interview process. Trying to determine what sort of answer will be pleasing to the audience is usually an exercise in futility. This is especially detrimental if the teacher is no longer staying true to her fundamental beliefs and convictions.

Any advice that a teacher takes to heart needs to be in keeping with her true identity. For example, a teacher may hear advice that teaching is a highly social profession and a candidate should come across as friendly and approachable. While this is certainly sound advice, a teacher should not internalize this advice to suggest that she should betray her own personality to make that impression.

If a teacher is a natural introvert, she should not try to pretend she is extraverted in her interview. Instead, she should attempt to be a warm and friendly introvert. The point is to highlight the best qualities of a person's genuine nature. A teacher should never adopt a disingenuous set of qualities to impress the group.

A teacher must remember that typically every candidate says nearly the same thing in an interview. Teachers fall into patterns of expected answers and many teams are hardly able to remember one candidate from another after a series of interviews throughout the day.

There are ways to be memorable to a hiring team without resorting to attention-seeking behaviors. Without changing the professional nature of the event, a teacher should try to make the interview feel more conversational. Interviews become exhausting in a hurry if the process feels like nothing more than preprepared questions answered by a string of candidates who all basically say the same thing. Making the interview feel like a conversation transforms the event.

For example, if a teacher were asked a question about the method she uses to prepare lessons, consider these two responses:

Teacher #1: I prepare my lessons after school every day reflecting on the successes and struggles of my students each day.

Teacher #2: That's a very important question you have asked. The work we are doing is too complex and important to begin without substantial preparation and planning.

The first teacher does not give a troubling answer. She certainly answers the question that is asked and does so in a way that helps the interview committee recognize the thoughtfulness that goes into her work each day. But would any candidate say something much different? Moreover, is there anything about the beginning of her answer that draws the committee members into the conversation?

The second teacher prefaces her comments by thanking the committee for asking such an astute question. This creates a connection between the interviewee and the team. Everyone agrees that they are asking the right questions. She continues her response by framing the reasons why the question is appropriate. After this lead-in, she will likely answer the question in a very similar way as the first teacher. However, the way she turns a standard, scripted interview question into a dialogue will be far more memorable.

In any conversation, no one remembers exactly what was said over time. To imagine that a hiring team will remember large pieces of an hour-long interview (when it will be followed by another four interviews just like it) is unreasonable. People remember small chunks of words and phrases and important ideas. Since the team will remember only small bits of the dialogue, teachers need to prepare answers that are memorable.

This can easily be accomplished in a teacher's preparatory work. These small sound bites need to be memorable but not cliché. For example, an overused phrase in education is "all students can learn." However noble the intention is behind a statement like this, educators have heard this phrase used so often it has nearly lost its meaning.

In contrast, "all students can learn" can be transformed slightly and create a more memorable idea for others to consider. Instead, a teacher could say, "We have all heard that all students can learn, but I feel like some have glossed over the significance of the word *all*. To me, all means all. When I am faced with the temptation that it is reasonable to exert my energies elsewhere, I remember that I made a promise. All means all."

If a teacher were to respond in this way, committee members would likely write, "All means all!" underlining it multiple times for emphasis. This is a line that is memorable because it is rooted in the heart. Teachers should steer clear from catch phrases and jargon that do not have strong personal connections to the teacher.

Within this spirit of honesty and a genuine desire to communicate the truth of the profession as they see it, teachers can begin answering the questions. Teachers should recall their preparation and consult their notes as needed to pull out the key ideas that they want to impart for each question.

In a thoughtful manner, the prospective teacher needs to build her case by citing stories and referring to genuine student work throughout the course of the questions. The stories and student work bring a level of authenticity to the answers. Anyone can claim to do powerful things in the classroom. Student artifacts and personal stories of successes in the classroom bring color to the black and white world of a formal interview setting.

In the end, the teacher wants to make an impression. This impression should be genuine and accurate. This impression should be honest and for all the right reasons. Typically, there are two ways that interview committee members talk about candidates after the interviews are over. When the principal asks the committee what they think of Ms. Turner, they will respond in one of the following ways:

Response #1: Ms. Turner? Which one was she? Was she the one in the red turtleneck or the one with the giant hoop earrings?

Response #2: Ms. Turner? Oh yeah, she's the one that told us about her student, Thomas. Man, I've had some students like him in my time. It sounds like she has made real progress with him. I thought it was especially powerful that she talked about how she has addressed his behavioral issues in class, but then also included his work when she talked about the academic gains students are making in her class. If she can get that kid squared away, I'm a believer. . . .

How will you be remembered? The committee will do the best with the material they are given. Teachers must bring substantial preparation to life in the context of the formal interview setting. Doing so makes all the difference.

The purpose of the interview is to communicate competence without seeming to be a know-it-all. The prospective teacher imparts her beliefs and acquired skills while acknowledging the need and desire to grow as a professional. The new teacher does not pretend to have mastery over the complexities of the profession. Suggesting that a sixteen-week student teaching experience has made one an expert is unwise.

Rather, the new teacher must project the message that she has capitalized upon every opportunity given to her thus far and has produced exemplary work because of it. At this point, the new teacher simply needs to be afforded the opportunity to continue her commitment to the profession by being hired to join in the work with other dedicated professionals. By portraying herself in this way, a hiring team is sure to accept her offer to serve their students.

Chapter 11

The Final Analysis

Beginning with events that started before entering the student teaching assignment, every action and decision has been squarely upon the shoulders of the student teacher to control and guide. The instant an interview is over, that all comes to an end. As soon as the candidate exchanges pleasantries with the team and thanks them for the opportunity to interview, the process is no longer in the teacher's hands. At this decisive juncture, the prospective teacher moves from having absolute control to having no control whatsoever.

The period of time between leaving the interview and waiting for an answer can be excruciating. The mind hops from all possibilities. *I think they liked my answers. Am I really going to be working here in a few months? I can't believe I blew the last question. Maybe they thought I was incompetent. I wonder if I will ever get a job?*

In these moments, it is hard for a prospective teacher to find a moment's peace. One way to combat the anxiety is to consider one basic question: Do the members of the hiring committee know who I really am?

This question should be at the heart of all answers that the candidate gave and should guide reflection moving forward. It is easy to slip into speculation of whether each question was answered with the proper nuance. Reflecting upon the interview in this way is an exercise in futility.

The decisions of the hiring team are not likely to be made with the excruciating analysis to which candidates are likely to subject themselves after the interview. Teachers should not be too hard on themselves regarding the minutiae of the interview. Even the most talented and seasoned teachers would not interview without stumbling occasionally.

Teachers should simply reflect on whether the answers given reflect their true beliefs and values. This is the essence of an interview and should guide a candidate's self-assessment of the interview. The reason that candidates need to be careful in how they reflect upon the interview is that their self-conception can often be damaged unnecessarily in the process.

Interview teams select the person who they believe best fills their needs. This process, however, is an imperfect science. Just as good, competent teachers are passed over every day, weak teachers are often selected in the position. The best candidate is not always the one who is chosen. As troubling as this may seem, it should reassure teachers who get passed over that they are not damaged goods.

There are many reasons why inferior teachers are selected. Unfortunately, some schools are led by weak leaders. Weak leaders often hire weak teachers. They may not recognize talent when they see it and they may not even prefer to hire the most talented educators. This can be due to principals who feel threatened by strong teachers. Strong teachers can often be strong willed and weak principals may select against these qualities. A teacher who intimidates a weak principal may be a teacher who is not selected for the position.

Other times, the principal may simply make a lazy hire. As difficult as it may be to imagine, some principals may only search through the list of candidates for the first four or five who seem qualified. Talented teachers with names at the end of the alphabet may not even secure an interview in these schools.

Principals may make their selection for several other troubling reasons. Sometimes teachers are hired who are not the best but are able to fill another void in the system. Unfortunately, needing to hire a football coach has resulted in subpar teachers securing a position over more talented peers.

Likewise, sometimes principals do not extend the proper time and energy to the hiring process. Whether summer break is looming or the principal is buried in discipline issues, the hiring process does not always receive the pride of place that it deserves on the to-do list of a busy administrator.

Of course, principals are also guilty of hiring those whom they know in a different capacity as well. When a principal sees a familiar name on the list of applicants, he may downshift his efforts to put together a rigorous process because he believes he has at least one candidate with whom "he can live."

These are unacceptable and detestable hiring practices but are certainly quite common nonetheless. The entire process of hiring is predicated on a committee selecting one person over all others. While candidates should hope that this process is done thoroughly and professionally, they have no control over the way in which it actually occurs.

Teachers interviewing for positions must not obsess over these possibilities nor be discouraged because of them. Rather, they should guard against personalizing the selection process in a way that makes them feel diminished if they are not selected.

On most occasions (hopefully), the team does hire the best candidate. Unfortunately, when this happens, it can also mean that they have selected someone else. It is important to recognize that this likely says more about the value system of the team than it does about the competency of the candidates.

Hiring teams extend interviews only to those they know are qualified for the job. Getting an interview is a strong testament of a prospective teacher's competency. This should not be undervalued. Candidates should take great pride in the value and dignity extended to them by being offered an interview.

However, only one person is ever selected for a position. This selection will depend upon the value system of the team. For example, if the principal considers the complement of the existing grade-level team in making the decision, she may decide to hire someone with a particular skill that brings balance to the skills of others. This candidate may not have the strongest skills in all areas of practice, but only in the area where the principal is focusing. One team may be looking for a candidate who understands performance data; another team may be searching for a candidate with a strong background in interventions for students.

For any given question, some of the hiring committee members may not be able to recognize quality answers even when they hear them. For example, if a guidance counselor is on the team, she may care deeply about the students but be unfamiliar with appropriate answers for content questions or best practices in assessment. Candidates should not overanalyze how they should have answered questions better knowing that the team members may not have fully understood the best answer a candidate could give for a question.

The qualities that separate the chosen candidate from others may have very little to with any overarching notion of "strongest candidate." Instead, the candidate chosen is the one who seemed to fit best within the team. Other qualities are important besides the fit within the grade-level team, but the principal may decide that this characteristic is more important than others in the selection process. Because of this, another candidate may be more qualified in some respects but just not in the area where the principal chose to focus the decision.

If a selection committee fails to value the strong qualities a candidate brings to the position, it is important for the candidate to decide whether working in that setting would have made sense anyway. If a principal does not value the unique combination of skills and behaviors that a teacher would bring to the job, that teacher would likely be miserable in the position even if she would have been hired.

One may make the assumption that there are a fixed number of qualities that a principal desires and each candidate interviewed falls somewhere along the spectrum of talent. In this scenario, the principal would simply rank all candidates and first place would naturally get the job. It simply does not work in this way.

For example, the teacher who gave a superior answer on classroom management may have given a subpar answer on a question about best instructional practices. Another candidate gave an exemplary answer to the question on instructional practices but a less than stellar answer to the question on student behavior. In this case, who should the principal select?

Aside from the fact that candidates do not always emerge as the best in every respect, there are always categories of questions that simply matter more to a principal. For example, if the school has a population of students that are failing to thrive academically, the principal may put more weight to a question about academic interventions than a question about lesson design.

Somehow, amid the wide variety of pressing matters of greatest importance and personal professional biases of the hiring committee, a candidate is chosen. For every person who sees wisdom in the decision, there are others who question the outcome of the process.

Prospective teachers can get so caught up in their desire to begin their teaching career that they forget to consider whether they may really want the job. At first blush, the answer seems quite obvious. The teacher has invested years of hard work and preparation into the culminating experience of securing a position. Why wouldn't a teacher accept the position?

The answer is not as obvious as it may seem. The teaching profession is exceptionally tough and grueling under the best circumstances. The sad reality is that not all school systems are healthy and functional. If a school is fundamentally disordered and dysfunctional, it can present extreme challenges for a new teacher. Teaching is too hard to work in any place but a great school or at least a school that wants to be great.

Great schools are primarily places where innovation and continuous growth are encouraged and expected. These schools are often particularly selective in the kinds of qualities they are seeking. Without question, great schools are not hiring average teachers. Because of this, novice teachers should certainly strive to land a position in a great school but should never feel ashamed if they are not selected for hire.

Aside from the dilemma of deciding to accept a position in a school that may not be completely healthy, there are also a few characteristics of schools that a candidate needs to consider in accepting a position. To begin, candidates must consider if they are willing to relocate to another place to begin their career. This can be tricky as teachers sometimes move away from all the supportive people in their lives as they begin a difficult professional transition. The loss of the proximity of family and friends is an important consideration that could affect a teacher's professional stability.

The Final Analysis

Other characteristics of a school can play into the decision-making process as well. Factors such as the size of the school, the age of students in the vacant position, subject matter of the teaching assignment, diversity in community population, and the socioeconomics of the school are real factors in how the school will operate. There is no preferable mix of these qualities, of course. Rather, candidates must discern whether any particular mix of these qualities would shape their decision in accepting the position. Schools come in every variety imaginable. Establishing some real clarity on what a candidate wants, or is willing to do, is important.

Teachers must consider whether they would accept any position that may be offered. There is a chance that teachers do not discover until the interview process that the school may be a challenging place to begin the profession. In reality, teachers are probably very excited to begin their careers and would not likely turn down a position if offered. In truth, teachers need to be very careful in applying for positions if they do not intend to accept them.

The point is not to dissuade teachers from accepting positions in difficult schools. However, it may bring some consolation for a teacher to recognize that failing to secure a position is not the end of the world. In fact, there are many other positions that may even be preferable.

At some point in everyone's professional career, they are faced with the reality of being rejected for a position. This is never a pleasant experience and can be handled in many ways. The candidate should accept the news they have been given with as much grace and poise as can be mustered under the circumstances. It is likely that the phone conversation breaking the news will not last very long, and it is critical for the candidate to maintain a level of professionalism throughout the conversation.

The teacher can never know if the principal will have another opening in the building or if the principal will pass along the candidate's name to other colleagues for potential jobs in the future. For these reasons, it is very important to maintain a professional demeanor despite the difficult news. The worst thing a teacher can do is burn a bridge very early in her professional career because of her disappointment.

When a principal makes the call to inform the candidate that the team has offered the position to someone else, the principal will not likely wish to speak very long. These calls are nearly as painful to make as they are to receive, and principals will usually be brief and blunt in relaying information to unsuccessful candidates.

Principals handle the calls in this manner for good reason. Because of the threat of legal action brought on by disgruntled candidates attempting to sue schools because they were not hired for positions, principals are reluctant to reveal any information that could be used against them.

This reality is very unfortunate for novice teachers. In fact, this is the reason why mock interviews can be so helpful. A mock interview is the only time a principal is likely to speak freely about the strengths and weaknesses of a candidate. If a student teacher can convince a principal to run through some interview questions, the teacher should be very grateful for the opportunity.

The following scenario is the typical call a prospective teacher will receive if she is not selected for a teaching position:

Principal: Hello, Madelyn. This is Mrs. Jackson from Wilson Elementary. I wanted to call and thank you for interviewing with us this morning. Unfortunately, I did need to let you know that we have offered the position to another candidate. We believe you did a very nice job and wish you the very best as you move forward.

Teacher: Can you tell me why I was not selected?

Principal: You are certainly a qualified candidate, Madelyn. That is why we extended you an interview. We believed that another candidate simply was a better fit for the position.

This conversation served the purpose the principal intended. That is, the candidate was informed of the decision without the principal revealing much information that could later be the source of objection. Unfortunately, the teacher has not learned much that can be helpful in future interview opportunities.

However, part of the reason why the teacher received that particular response was because of the way she asked the question, "Can you tell me why I was not selected?" When the question is phrased in this way, it immediately asks for a comparison between the teacher and the candidate who was selected. Principals will avoid sharing this sort of information with the teacher. Further, it simply provides the principal with the escape hatch answer ("The other candidate was a better fit"). This answer is a standard response from principals and asking a question that elicits it will likely limit the conversation immediately. Instead, the teacher should reframe the question in a way that may elicit a different response:

Teacher: Can you tell me one or two things I can work on to be considered a stronger candidate moving forward?

This is an entirely different question. The principal cannot retreat under cover by referencing the "fit" of the other candidate. Also, it is not asking the principal to describe the reasons why the candidate did not secure the position. This is a critical distinction. Instead, the candidate is merely asking for a couple of helpful suggestions.

This is a question that requires bravery. If a candidate chooses to ask this question, she must be prepared to hear the answer. The answer may, in fact, hurt. No one likes to hear criticism especially when the answers that are given are the likely reasons why the candidate was unsuccessful as a professional.

If the principal chooses to give the candidate feedback at this point, it is a precious, if not painful, gift. Because of the emotion tied up with the conversation, the candidate is not likely to remember the details as the sting of rejection wears off. Because of this, the teacher should jot down the suggestions as notes to read at another time. The candidate will not be able to internalize valuable feedback while trying to process disappointment.

Teachers should reflect upon the feedback they are given very carefully. A teacher's first instinct may be to dismiss the criticism and think of times and occasions where the criticism is not valid. This is a mistake.

When a principal describes a quality or skill that seemed deficient, the principal is not concluding that the candidate does not possess it. Rather, the principal is truthfully relaying the factual information that the quality did not come across *during* the interview. For example, if the principal suggests that the teacher seemed to lack an understanding of formative assessment, the principal is not claiming that the teacher is deficient in this area of preparation. Rather, the principal is relaying that the teacher did not *demonstrate* that understanding.

There is a world of difference between perception and reality at times. However, the hiring team's perception is the only thing they can judge. While it is important for teachers to possess requisite skills for a job, it is also important that they communicate this competency as well. A candidate may be able to argue underlying ability but can never argue the perception that was generated in the interview.

At times, candidates will need to brush up on their skill set. On other occasions, they must rethink the way in which they came across in the interview. Regardless of the nature of the feedback the teacher may receive, reflecting deeply upon the suggestions and implications is an important next step as the teacher regroups for the next opportunity.

Incorporating suggestions from the feedback received in this process can only serve to strengthen the skills that the teacher will bring into the next rounds of interviews. However, teachers must also guard against the inevitable damage that can be caused when they are unsuccessful in the interview process.

Everyone finds rejection difficult to process, but this is exacerbated by the way in which educators tend to blend who they are with what they do for a living. Some believe that failing to be selected for a position is not just an indictment against the teacher's skill set, but against who the person is as a human being.

This can be very difficult to separate. Failure to secure a teaching position is not the same as failing as an educator. Moreover, failure to secure a teaching position is not synonymous with failing as a person. A teacher must ask, "If failing to secure this position does not question my fundamental worth, what else could this mean?"

Teachers must make conscientious decisions to de-personalize their analysis of the interview process. By focusing on areas of improvement and refinement, the candidate can reapply for new jobs with the added confidence that she will bring in all of her former strong qualities plus the new additional modifications she has received as feedback.

Teachers must be deliberate in staying focused throughout this process. The human mind is able to process rejection in a healthy way, but there are many negative ways in which a person can begin to view the situation.

Primarily, rejection can cause a person to question his own self-worth. *Has the committee revealed that I am indeed a fraud? Maybe I don't have what it takes to become a teacher. Maybe this is a sign that this isn't my path.*

Allowing the mind to wander in these directions is to read far more into the selection process than good sense would warrant. Hiring committees do their best to select one person out of many to fill their need. There is nothing baked into that process that would suggest that all others are weak.

History provides a strong example of just how strong a second-place finisher can be. Most people have heard of the celebrated Triple Crown winner, Affirmed. However, another legendary horse raced in all three of the Triple Crown races as well. His name was Alydar. In the 1978 Kentucky Derby, Affirmed and Alydar raced against each other and Affirmed prevailed by a mere one and a half lengths. A few weeks later, they again raced and Affirmed was once again the victor by "a neck." Just under a month later, they met for the third race of the Triple Crown at the Belmont Stakes. Many would suggest that this rivalry may have provided the most compelling race in all of sport's history when they battled it out for one and a half miles. Affirmed won that race as well finishing ahead of Alydar "by a head."

Affirmed was an amazing race horse, but so was Alydar. If Affirmed would not have run that year, Alydar would have been a Triple Crown winner. In all three races, Alydar came up a bit short. But Alydar was an incredible and magnificent race horse in his own right. He went on to sire many championship horses as part of his legacy. Second place does not indicate weakness.

Rejection also can cause a person to feel like they have lost their sense of belonging. When people decide to enter the teaching profession, it defines who they are. This can be very difficult for a person who desperately wants to be defined as a teacher but has not yet accepted a teacher position.

A teacher is a "do-er." If one is not able to engage in the act of teaching, that person feels like she does not yet have full acceptance into the professional community. Feeling like an outsider in the very way that most defines them can be very distressing to teachers.

Being rejected for a teaching position can also cause a person to process that situation in another negative way. Because the selection process is outside of the candidate's hands, a fear of powerlessness can descend upon the teacher. The mind can begin to feel as if the powers that be are failing to appreciate the knowledge and skill that the teacher could bring to the classroom. This can make a person lash out in anger. *Who do they think they are? As if they even know what a good teacher looks like! Have you seen some of the teachers on that staff? Are you telling me the process isn't rigged?*

This response can be the most destructive of all. Questioning one's own self-worth or becoming distraught over a desire to belong to a group can be destructive, and this emotional response may result in the candidate saying or doing something that will later be regretted.

It is difficult to feel powerless in a situation of personal importance. However, candidates must channel that emotional energy into a positive investment in themselves. Instead of lashing out at others, teachers can spend time refining and adjusting aspects of their paperwork and practice to ensure better results in the future. If prospective employers hear that a candidate responds emotionally to the news that she didn't get a position, it will reaffirm their decision that the candidate lacks emotional control and that reputation may sabotage attempts to be hired in the future.

Rejection does not respond well to reason. Rejection elicits an emotional response of one type or another. Candidates must guard against expressing any negativity to others. They have nothing to gain and a lot to lose by vocalizing their hurt. Once the teacher can process the emotion behind the rejection, rational thoughts and decisions must be the proactive way in which the teacher regroups.

To escape endless mental loops, teachers should put their thoughts in writing. On the top of the page, the teacher should write, "What did I learn from this experience?" By listing both the feedback received from the principal and the teacher's own observations about the experience, a list can be assembled that is of value:

I forgot everyone's name during the interview. I could have drawn a rectangle on the paper in my notebook and jotted down the names by where they were sitting around the table.

My palms were so sweaty. I am going to put tissues in my pocket, so I can dry them off before shaking everyone's hand.

The question about pedagogy threw me off. I don't know as much as I thought I do about instructional practices. I need some more concrete examples.

I botched the differentiated instruction question. My answer only said that teachers should vary their practices, but I didn't give examples.

The principal said I may want to work more on giving concise answers. I think I started rambling. I could time myself answering practice questions, limiting myself to only four minutes per answer.

When a teacher can begin viewing the experience from a rational point of view and can look for solutions, new insights will come. Above all, the teacher does not need to become a new or better person. Instead, the teacher simply needs to express her greatness in more effective ways.

As a teacher regroups for the next round of possible interviews, she should keep busy in ways that can add to her experience and expertise. For example, teachers should consider substitute teaching whenever their schedules allow. Not only does this give a teacher more professional experiences to build teaching skills, but it also provides additional experience that can be added to a resume.

If the teacher is unable to secure a teaching position at all for the upcoming year, she needs to consider the options that may be available to continue building professional experiences. In addition to regular substitute teaching, schools often seek long-term substitutes for teachers on maternity leave or for those who require a leave of absence.

Additionally, some recent graduates choose to apply for jobs as paraprofessional teaching assistants. Teachers should not assume that this will type cast them into a position that will preclude them from attaining a teaching position in the future. Many teachers begin their careers as para-educators. It has shown to be a proving ground where teaching talents emerge and are noticed by other teachers and administrators.

Timing is everything. Teachers need to do everything within their control to position themselves to be the most desirable candidate. The rest is a process that others control. Continuing to work actively to refine abilities as both a teacher and an interviewee is the work of the teacher seeking a position. Remaining relentless in that pursuit is the minimum expectation.

There is a lot of hard work that goes into both becoming a teacher and preparing for the interview process. This hard work is worth it. The hard work represents the culminating efforts of a lifelong dream and years of study and practice. Teachers must remain positive and productive throughout the entire experience.

At the end of the road, there is a payoff. The payoff comes in many forms. Of course, there is a financial payoff when one becomes employed, which provides needed security in life. Getting out from under the debt that can often be accrued in college is on the minds of most young teachers.

There is also the payoff in accomplishing a professional goal. Setting the mind to a goal over the course of many years by chipping away at the requirements is fulfilling. It is understandable that a teacher does not feel like the last summit has been achieved until she signs her first contract. Walking into a classroom for the first time that has your name on the door is incredibly rewarding.

However, there is a far greater payoff. Entire classrooms are full of students who need help. There are kids across this nation who desperately need a talented and devoted teacher. A teacher can change everything in a young person's life. Like a lock that holds fast until one very specific key opens it, teachers can be the one deciding factor that opens up a child in ways previously unimagined.

The world needs great teachers more than ever. The time is now to revolutionize the world of a child. Summon up all of your energy and talent and go find the children who are desperately waiting. Do everything in your power. If necessary, go break down the schoolhouse doors to find them.

About the Author

Dr. Stephen V. Newton has worked as a teacher, school administrator, and academic professional at the K–12, college, and university levels for over twenty-four years. He currently serves as the Director of Curriculum and Instruction for the local school district in Cheyenne, Wyoming. He also serves as an educational consultant focused on leadership development, data analysis, postsecondary readiness, and literacy. Stephen is married to Amanda, an attorney, and has been blessed with six wonderful children.

www.ingramcontent.com/pod-product-compliance
Lightning Source LLC
Chambersburg PA
CBHW021845220426
43663CB00005B/416